LIVING LIFE 2 TH

NEVER FORGOTTEN

KERRY KERR MCAVOY, PhD

© 2020 Kerry Kerr McAvoy

All rights reserved. No part of this publication may be reproduced, stored in a retrieval system, or transmitted in any form or by any means—for example, electronic, photocopy, recording—without the prior written permission of the copyright owner.
This book was formerly published under the title of *Pain as a Starting Point*

ISBN: 9798553382445

Scriptures taken from the Holy Bible, New International Version®, NIV®. Copyright © 1973, 1978, 1984, 2011 by Biblica, Inc.™ Used by permission of Zondervan. All rights reserved worldwide.www.zondervan.com The "NIV" and "New International Version" are trademarks registered in the United States Patent and Trademark Office by Biblica, Inc.™

Cover Photo by Sharon McCutcheon
Printed in the United States of America

Dedications

I dedicate this book to two people who have been very instrumental in this project. First to my late husband, Brad, for his continuing belief, patience, support, and faith. He was often my first reader and best cheerleader. I could have begun the journey of writing without his belief and encouragement.

And to my friend Chris, who looked at me with puzzlement when I announced I planned to start writing fiction instead of devotionals and quipped, "That would be a loss!" Thanks for the prodding!

Finally, I remember with my precious, beloved dog of nine years, Zoe, who unexpectedly passed during the writing of this book. She is missed.

CONTENT

Acknowledgments 5

Introduction 7

Chapter 1
Mysterious & Good God 11

Chapter 2
When Life Doesn't Make Sense 35

Chapter 3
Psychological Need for God 55

Chapter 4
Comfort in God 83

Conclusion 113

Sources ....
117

Acknowledgments

A book is never written in isolation. It is birthed out of conversations between friends and colleagues, out of heated debates with family members, and by absorbing the exciting ideas of others' inspirational sermons, lectures, and writings. It comes through a combination of fun flashes, of "ah-ha's" and the sheer drudgery of forcing yourself to sit and stare at the computer until words appear on the screen. In other words, writing a book is a process.

And in the process of writing this book, many people have been instrumental. I want to first thank my parents who instilled in me the belief that anything is possible. I wish my dad were here to celebrate this book being published, but I suspect he sees and knows about it. My husband, Brad, was amazingly supportive. He put up with my strange hours, reading and editing my work, and listening to me struggle with various psychological and biblical concepts. I thank my children for being patient with me. Cameron, Devon, and Kellin's support has meant the world to me. I am very lucky to have such talented young men for sons.

Editors are a critical part of the process. They have to walk the difficult line of being truthful yet tactful. Thanks to Hannah Max for looking over the first draft. Mary Wendt, the second editor, took the work and challenged me to dig deeper. I thank her for her honesty, which had the right measure of criticalness and gentleness. Her feedback encouraged to me to re-think some of my points and conclusions. This book is much stronger for her involvement.

Then I want to thank those special friends who have inspired me. Cameron and Jill Warne encouraged me to put more of myself into this work. Their quiet support has been invaluable. Being familiar in the creative process themselves, they understood the challenges that were involved in the writing of this book. I also want to thank Chris Kanai who calls herself my first and biggest fan. I have appreciated our conversations around this book. I thank her for challenging me when she thought the work was too vague or muddy. She often offered interesting thoughts that sent me into better directions.

I appreciate my initial readers, Dr. John Frye and Dr. Kevin Baird, two wonderful pastors and theologians. Their feedback was very valuable and encouraging. I also want to thank my beta readers: Ann MacDonald, Katie Kiger, Erica Christoff, Rachel Pickard, Scott Kanai, Josh VanTil, Lisa Watson, Deb DeGroot, Colleen DeGraaf, Jake Houf, Laurie Johnson, Theresa Steele, Jennifer Balcom, Dana Balcom, Katy Spengler, Wayne Nelson, Dawn Longcore, Patti Kenyon, Dr. David Crump, Daile Zink, and Cameron Warne for their comments and input.

Introduction

My last day of work before Christmas vacation had been a busy one. With the car full of groceries, I pulled into my driveway and let out a sigh of relief. All that was left for me to do was put away the items I had bought and make dinner.

As I turned off the ignition, I looked up to see my 12-year-old son racing out of the house. "Zoe's been hit! Zoe's been hit by a car!" he screamed.

Rushing into the house, I found my dog lying limp on the backroom floor. Blood oozed with each rattling breath. She seemed lifeless, near death. Her back leg was crooked and floppy, obviously broken.

All three of my boys moved into action and helped to unload the bags of groceries while I called the Emergency Animal Hospital. My eldest son and I lifted Zoe's fifty-pound body into the back seat while the other two boys jumped into the car.

"What happened?" I asked as we headed to the vet's office.

Devon spoke up. "I was taking the garbage can out to the curb, and I let Zoe come with me."

"Without a leash?"

He looked guilty as tears fell down his cheeks. "Yes," he said. "I didn't know she would run into the road. I yelled and told her to come back but she ran right in front of a car!"

I looked back at Zoe. Her breaths were getting louder and now had a rattily, raspy quality.

"Listen guys, this is really bad. She may not make it. And if she dies, we will be turning around and going home."

The tension and fear grew palpable in the car. At each stoplight Devon began to chant under his breath, "Please be green! Please be green!" His face was tight with tension as we waited at each red light.

I knew Devon adored Zoe. Recently he had been helping me train her. Images of him witnessing our family dog being struck by a car flashed through my head; I felt sick to my stomach. "How will this impact him if Zoe dies?" I wondered.

Glancing at him, I saw that his shoulders were stooped over and shaking with his sobs.

I joined my children's quiet chant. Instead of repeating "please be green!" as we drove up to each stop light, I silently prayed, "Please don't let Zoe die. The guilt and blame will deeply wound my son if our dog dies. Please, God, please don't let Zoe die!"

Zoe came home a few days later, just in time to be with our family on Christmas Eve. It was the best Christmas gift I received that year because I knew both my dog and my son would recover.

God answered my prayer that day, but there have been plenty of times when I haven't gotten the response I wanted. Sometimes God says no. As a psychologist, I have come to the realization through my counseling experiences that suffering is an inescapable part of our lives. Pain can come in many forms. Sometimes it is subtle and chronic, and other times it tears us apart with its cruelty and finality.

When we suffer, we often struggle to understand God. He might seem distant or unavailable. We begin to wonder if God has left us on our own. We question whether or not God sees our problem and pain. And, we wonder if he knows about our situation. We ask, "Does he care?"

God, however, promises never to leave nor forsake us. We are *not forgotten*. Instead, he longs to equip us with the confidence and faith to face life's uncertainties. Like Job, we may find life's trials offer us an opportunity to rediscover and renew our faith. It can provide an opportunity to challenge our assumptions about what we believe. We may wonder: does life or God owe us anything? Can we really trust in God and his promises when we face challenges? How will we react emotionally to pain? Time of hardship can drive us to search for a deeper relationship with God.

Each chapter of this devotional includes an introduction to the topic, and a weekly opener to a meditation or spiritual discipline practice, followed by five days of devotional reading. There is a rich tradition of spiritual practices in the Christian life such as fasting, Bible study, prayer, worship, and meditation. The format of this study is designed to encourage you to engage in a variety of these disciplines since a healthy spiritual relationship depends on our full participation.

You will also notice that instead of traditionally-styled questions found in most Bible studies, psychological questions are used in this book. The purpose of these questions is to help you engage with the material in a different way. It can be challenging to change our common attitudes and behaviors unless we understand the underlying reasons for our actions. The psychological questions in this study are intended to help you explore your basic assumptions. Through the use of the material, you may discover inconsistencies between what is believed to be true and what is practiced in one's day-to-day life. An increased awareness of such discrepancies can enable you to address areas of disbelief thus improving your spiritual life.

This study contains four chapters. The first chapter explores prevalent misperceptions about God. For example, even though we know he is mysterious, omnipotent, and sovereign, we often assume he will behave in predictable and familiar ways. In the second chapter you will see that pain is a frequent theme in the Bible and explore five common biblical explanations for it. The third chapter shifts gears and explores your psychological need for God. You will discover we have been intentionally designed to require care and attention from God but often fail to recognize this hunger as a spiritual need. Instead, we attempt to address our need by pursuing our careers and addictions, financial gain, notoriety or sex. In the final chapter you will explore how to depend on the person and character of God. It isn't enough to know God understands your psychological needs; you need to actively seek him for aid and comfort. A working faith requires us to pursue God, to trust in him, to obey his commands, to abide or *remain* in him, and to have hope. By working through this study, you will find that God's plan for our lives is good, despite painful circumstances.

God is your most passionate lover. Right now he is waiting for you to seek him out so that he can give you comfort. You are not alone. You never have been. In this study you will discover that if you feel alienated from God, it is due to common misperceptions that have caused this sense of separation from God. God hasn't left you. He is here—right by your side. Suffering doesn't need to separate you farther from God; instead it can act as an opportunity to discover that you've never been forgotten.

Chapter 1

Mysterious & Good God

*"For my thoughts are not your thoughts,
  neither are your ways my ways,"
  declares the Lord.
"As the heavens are higher than the earth,
  so are my ways higher than your ways
  and my thoughts than your thoughts.
As the rain and the snow
  come down from heaven,
and do not return to it
  without watering the earth
and making it bud and flourish,
  so that it yields seed for the sower and bread for the eater,
so is my word that goes out from my mouth:
  It will not return to me empty
but will accomplish what I desire
  and achieve the purpose for which I sent it."*

Isaiah 55:8–11

My first two pregnancies were rough. Each time, I was diagnosed with preeclampsia which required mandatory bed rest for the final few weeks. If that wasn't enough, both labors had failed to progress, resulting in surgical deliveries. I was now pregnant with my third child and wanted a better experience. With two busy boys at home and a third one on the way, I needed to bounce back quickly after this labor and delivery.

For some irrational reason, I latched on to God's words to Eve: "I will make your pains in childbearing very severe; with painful labor you will give birth to children" (Genesis 3:16). I wondered if I could find a way around this declaration. Could I ask God for a painless, easy labor and delivery? What must I do to earn that kind of experience? As I wrestled with this issue, I began to ask God to have mercy on me and to save me from the previous difficulties of the first two pregnancies.

God, however, said no. By the latter part of my second trimester, my blood pressure was soaring and my heart was racing. The constant pounding in my chest made it difficult to sleep at night. I felt light-headed and weak while grocery shopping or preparing my family meals. Each night, I fell into bed exhausted and wondered how I would be able to get up and take care of my five- and three-year-old sons. Although medication controlled the worst of the symptoms, my face, hands, and feet began to swell. Doctor visits were scheduled more often than normal as they medically prepared me for an early delivery.

I continued to cry out to God, "Lord, please give me a normal pregnancy and an easy labor! What must I do so that you will take this hardship away from me?" I wondered if God was testing my loyalty to him. In the midst of this I found Job's words helpful and began to pray them, "Though he slay me, yet will I hope in [him]" (Job 13:15). I slowly relinquished my desire for control over this situation and found comfort in Job's cry.

Miraculously the due date arrived, and labor was induced. After the first ten hours of labor, things turned for the worse. A monitor's alarm suddenly went off, alerting medical staff that my unborn baby's heart rate was plummeting with every contraction. Nothing helped.

Turning me over, having me sit up—each new effort failed to correct the situation. I was frantic. I knew my baby was slowly suffocating.

The medical staff moved into action, and a few minutes later, my youngest son was born, limp, lifeless, and with a deep purplish-black skin tone. My heart sank as I held my breath and waited for his first cry. It felt like an eternity before I finally heard him wail.

Despite coming home with a healthy baby, the experience of that pregnancy left me spiritually wounded. Although I was glad that my youngest son and I had survived a very dangerous situation, I wondered why I had to suffer. Why was my body, particularly my heart, weak? I wanted to be a better mother to my older two sons, yet I barely coped during the final months of my pregnancy. Did God care so little for me? For my boys? As a faithful Christian, I previously thought I had a right to lead a good life, but now I wasn't so sure. I was also coming to the realization that I didn't know God as well as I thought I did.

What I didn't understand at the time was that God is not like us. And, like many clients in my counseling practice, I felt disappointed. When we get into a difficult situation, we often pray for God's help. However when his intervention doesn't come in expected ways, we begin to doubt whether he cares. We begin to believe that he is either absent or inadequate. What we fail to understand is that his thoughts are not like our thoughts, and his ways are not our ways (Isaiah 55:8). He doesn't have our perspective, and he doesn't operate under the same principles we do. He also is not driven by emotional needs, unfulfilled goals, or a desire for personal achievement like we are.

We are especially frustrated when we discover God's main objective isn't our happiness but rather our holiness. It isn't that God doesn't want us happy, but rather he won't support our version of happiness. He knows true joy can only be achieved through intimacy with him, not by obtaining the good life. The difference in goals, however, can cause us to feel as if we are at cross-purposes with God.

Instead, we prefer God to be predictable and pliable. We wish he would behave like our lucky rabbit's foot and stay in our pocket until we need him to act on our behalf. He knows, though, that we will only find soul-satisfying pleasure through fellowship with him, and he will do whatever it takes to get us there, even if it means shattering our dreams. Like it or not, God doesn't follow your rules, and, in fact, he tells us he isn't like you at all.

So, who is God? What does the Bible tell us about him? As you explore God's mysterious nature, you will see what the Scriptures have to say about him. You will be able to examine your beliefs about God and see how consistent they are with the truth. And through this process, you will be encouraged to challenge your definitions of God, allowing you to meet him in new and more fulfilling ways.

OPENING QUESTIONS

Has there been a time when you felt disappointed or confused by God?

Using three adjectives, how would you describe God today?

Would your descriptions of God have been different 10 years ago?

How has time changed your perspective?

When you get into a difficult situation, what do you expect from God?

WEEKLY DISCIPLINE INTRODUCTION

Lectio divina is a meditation practice that focuses on Scripture readings and prayer. Each daily devotional in this chapter will have a different suggestion of Scriptural passages for this exercise, but you might want to use Isaiah 55:8–11 as the primary one. Read the suggested verses aloud, slowly, and with careful attention. Ask God to speak to you through his word. Re-read the passage. What verse or verses stand out to you? Listen to what God is saying to you through the passages. You may want to journal your insights.

DAY 1

No Other

You were shown these things so that you might know that the Lord is God; besides him there is no other.

Acknowledge and take to heart this day that the Lord is God in heaven above and on the earth below. There is no other.

Deuteronomy 4:35, 39

Two common misunderstandings concerning God's uniqueness cause us to see him as weak or powerless. We either over-estimate evil's potential, or we ignore God by relying on ourselves. Both relegate our omnipotent God to a lesser position and diminish his sovereignty.

The first error of over-estimating evil can be seen in some Hollywood movies. In these types of films, God or the forces of good usually are in a contest against evil. A wildly popular horror film, *Paranormal Activity*, fits this example. The story is about a young couple who are experiencing terrifying supernatural activity in their home. They unsuccessfully reach out for help and are eventually overpowered by dark forces. This perspective sees evil as God's evenly matched opponent and the outcome of the battle as uncertain.

The second error occurs when we ignore God by failing to turn to him first when making decisions or addressing needs or by living as if there is no God. In this scenario, God is absent from our lives. We live either as if his existence doesn't matter or as if he is too impotent to be counted on in times of trouble. We also tend to forget he isn't human by attributing our imperfect qualities of humanity to him. We figure he will be flaky or inconsistent like the other people in our lives. As a result we either don't turn to him at all, figuring he can't help us, or we beg and plead him for aid, as if he is a reluctant rescuer who has to be convinced.

These two attitudes fail to consider the nature of God. He is not frail, impotent, or inconsistent. His power is unparalleled and unmatched. In Deuteronomy, after Moses reviewed all the great things God had done for the Israelites, he ended his speech by reminding the people that God had shown evidence of his great power so that they would know his uniqueness. He said, "There is no other" (Deuteronomy 4:39). Through Moses, God revealed that he is unlike anything or anyone else—in all of creation or outside of creation.

God is a mystery and unfathomable, and his essence is holy. Moses asked to see God's glory, but it was so completely overwhelming that God had to cover Moses with his hand until he passed by him (Exodus 33:18–21). When Isaiah had a vision of God on his throne, he cried out that he was "ruined" (Isaiah 6:5). Both of these men learned that God's nature is glorious and unfathomable.

God's nature does not need to frighten or make you uncomfortable. In fact, your apprehension reveals your lack of understanding. God longs to address your misconceptions. He did so by giving us Jesus Christ (Hebrews 1:3), who, although he was divine, came to Earth in a human form so that you could know God (Philippians 2:6–8). The question is this: will you be open to getting to know him?

- Why do you think some people minimize God's power and uniqueness?

- Remember a recent time you faced trouble and recall how you viewed God. Did you find yourself begging and pleading, or did you forget to turn to him for help? What experiences might have shaped your opinion about God's desire to intervene on your behalf?

- Why might you resist getting to know God better by spending time in prayer and reading his word??

OPTIONAL READING

Isaiah 40:25–31

DAILY DISCIPLINE EXERCISE

Read Isaiah 40:25–31. Isaiah was writing words of encouragement to the Israelites as they were being exiled to Babylon.

PRAYER

Dear God, You have no equal. I cannot compare you to anyone. Help this truth become more real to me. Increase my desire to know you better.

DAY 2

Unchanging

In the beginning you laid the foundations of the earth,
  and the heavens are the work of your hands.
They will perish, but you remain;
  they will all wear out like a garment.
Like clothing you will change them
  and they will be discarded.
But you remain the same,
  and your years will never end.

Psalm 102:25–27

About the time we think we have all of life's rules figured out, we will once again be surprised. Probably the only consistent rule we can count on is to expect change. Facing change is one of the most frequent conversations that occur in my counseling office. Most of us dislike uncertainty and work to avoid it. We often stay at terrible jobs, are reluctant to break up with dysfunctional friends, lovers, or spouses, and avoid moving to a new city or state despite its better offerings.

Why do most of us dislike change? I suspect it has to do with our internal regulatory system which is on the constant lookout for any sign of possible danger or threat. Since we don't know what change will bring, the unknown feels risky and potentially frightening. Even when unhappy, we will often stay with what we know because it is familiar and we understand the threats it poses to us.

The Israelites made the unfortunate error of choosing the unpleasant familiar circumstances over the unknown yet possibly better future. Despite experiencing God's dramatic care as they traveled through the desert, the Israelites feared taking possession of the promised land of Canaan. Out of the twelve spies who visited the new territory, only two felt confident that with God's help they could face the new challenge. The other ten reported, "We went into the land to which you sent us, and it does flow with milk and honey! Here is its fruit. The people who live there are powerful, and the cities are fortified and very large" (Numbers 13:27–28a). Moses tried dissuading the people of their fears. He reminded them, "If the Lord is pleased with us, he will lead us into that land, a land flowing with milk and honey, and will give it to us. Only do not rebel against the Lord. And do not be afraid of the people of the land, because we will swallow them up. Their protection is gone, but the Lord is with us. Do not be afraid of them" (Numbers 14:8–9). Despite Moses' encouraging words, the Israelites failed to listen. And after the people rebelled and sided with the fearful ten spies, God denied everyone, except for the two spies who gave a positive report, entrance to the new lands. They spent the next forty years just outside of God's promised home, regretting their faithless decision.

What makes this story especially tragic is that the Israelites had witnessed God sending the ten plagues and parting the Red Sea. He fed them manna and quail, and personally traveled with them in the form of a cloud and fire, yet when it came to facing something scary, their fear loomed larger than God's faithfulness and strength. They forgot a very important fact: God is unchanging. He is the same today and tomorrow as he was yesterday. They should have known that if God was faithful, omnipotent, omnipresent, and sovereign before, then they could trust that he will be the same when they faced the difficult task of conquering new territories.

Aren't we just like the Israelites? Don't difficult circumstances and unknown conditions also make us forget who God is and his capabilities?

God's unchanging character can be a huge source of comfort to us. In his book, *The Knowledge of the Holy*, A.W. Tozer wrote, "God cannot change for the better. Since He is perfectly holy, He has never been less holy than He is now and can never be holier than He is and has always been. Neither can God change for the worse. Any deterioration within the unspeakably holy nature of God is impossible."[1] We do not need to wonder if God is moody. He is never unpredictable. He will act with the same level of integrity today and as he did yesterday. He cannot be compromised or manipulated. His love for us doesn't waver and it doesn't depend on our faithfulness or our goodness. God is immutable. As the author of Hebrews reminds, "Jesus Christ is the same yesterday and today and forever" (Hebrews 13:8). Life may be constantly changing, but you can take comfort in the fact that no matter your circumstances, our unchanging God is with you.

- Are you a person who likes or dislikes change? Explain your preference.

- Is there something in your life that needs addressing and might require some type of change?

- What is getting in the way of you dealing with this issue?

- Do you believe that God doesn't change? What is your reaction to the unchanging nature of God?

- How does this affect your relationship with him?

OPTIONAL READING

James 1:17

DAILY DISCIPLINE EXERCISE

Read Psalm 102. Although it is unclear who authored this set of passages, it is known as the *prayer of the afflicted.*

PRAYER

Dear God, Everything changes. Even I am not consistently the same. It is comforting to know that you are the same today as you were yesterday. This gives me confidence to face my future and to experience peace as I deal with today's issues. Thank you for being my rock, especially when I face the unknown.

DAY 3

Safe

No one is like you, Lord;
  you are great,
  and your name is mighty in power.
Who should not fear you,
  King of the nations?
  This is your due.
Among all the wise leaders of the nations
  and in all their kingdoms,
  there is no one like you.
They are all senseless and foolish;
  they are taught by worthless wooden idols.
Hammered silver is brought from Tarshish
  and gold from Uphaz.
What the craftsman and goldsmith have made
  is then dressed in blue and purple—
  all made by skilled workers.
But the Lord is the true God;
  he is the living God, the eternal King.
When he is angry, the earth trembles;

Jeremiah 10:6–10

In a wonderful scene in C.S. Lewis' book, *The Lion, The Witch, and The Wardrobe*, Lucy asked Mr. Beaver if Aslan, the roaring lion, was safe. She had encountered him and found his appearance frightening. She worried he might be dangerous.

"Safe?" said Mr. Beaver. "Don't you hear what Mrs. Beaver tells you? Who said anything about safe? 'Course he isn't safe. But he's good. He's the King, I tell you.'"[2]

Many of us are like Lucy. We get uncomfortable when we think about God being all-powerful and all-knowing. We wonder how *safe* God is.

It is not unusual for us to substitute our nature for God's nature. The early Greek gods and goddesses had human flaws, such as irrational anger, greed, and jealousy. Their personalities were a reflection of us. We do the same thing with God. Since we often are unreliable or have ulterior motives, we may unconsciously fear an all-powerful God and consider him dangerous.

We also are uneasy with the idea of his sovereignty and wonder if it threatens our free will. How we can be in charge of our destiny if God is in command? And, if his authority is perfect, why doesn't he predictably meet our expectations? Why do we have to experience painful circumstances? It is difficult to understand the balance between God allowing us to be our own free agents and his sovereign rule over all things. The insensibility of this paradox leaves us with questions.

God reveals in his word that he ultimately accomplishes what he desires (Isaiah 55:11) and that one day all will perfectly conform to his will (Revelation 21:1–4). The psalmist David understood this very well. He wrote, "O Lord, you have searched me and you know me. You know when I sit and when I rise; you perceive my thoughts from afar. You discern my going out and my lying down; you are familiar with all my ways. Before a word is on my tongue you know it completely, O Lord. You hem me in behind and before; you have laid your hand upon me" (Psalm 139:1–5). David did not find God's sovereignty threatening. His descriptions of God's actions are filled with warmth and affection which suggest he found God's omnipotence comforting. David's habit of spending time with God allowed him to know God's motives. He knew God's sovereignty was nothing to be feared.

God is working all things out according to his will (Ephesians 1:8b–10) and for the good of those who love him (Romans 8:28). From our limited perspective his actions will not always make sense, but, like David, you will be able to trust in God's sovereignty as you come to know him better.

- What is your reaction to God having a grand purpose and will?

- Is this concept threatening to you? If so, what makes it uncomfortable or feel unsafe?

- Give an example when you have seen God work a difficult situation out for you.

OPTIONAL READING
Psalm 139

DAILY DISCIPLINE EXERCISE
Read Psalm 139. David celebrated God's powerfulness and his constant presence in our lives.

PRAYER
Dear God, You are my Almighty Father. Sometimes I find the idea of your sovereignty uncomfortable. Make me more like the psalmist, David, who accepted and embraced your plan for his life.

DAY 4

Good

The Lord is gracious and compassionate,
　slow to anger and rich in love.
The Lord is good to all;
　he has compassion on all he has made.
The Lord is trustworthy in all his promises
　and faithful in all he does.
The Lord upholds all who fall
　and lifts up all who are bowed down.
The eyes of all look to you
　and you give them their food at the proper time.
You open your hand
　and satisfy the desires of every living thing.

Psalm 145:8–9,13b–16

Several years ago I had a crisis of faith. I had just had my last child, my career had hit its stride, and we had moved into our dream home. For all intents and purposes, we had achieved the American Dream. I, however, had hit an emotional wall. I was unhappy, discontented, and exhausted. What was wrong? My marriage was good. I had three beautiful, busy boys, and my career was going strong.

I remember standing in front of my kitchen sink, looking out of the window at my flower garden, and weeping. As I cried, I thought, "Why am I crying? I don't feel sad. What is going on with me?" And as I stood there, I realized I wasn't sure why God loved me. Was it because of my intelligence, my skills and talents, or because of my volunteer activities? Did being a good mom make God happier with me? I realized I had mistakenly thought my actions and efforts compelled

God to love me. Then I wondered, "What if I stopped doing all these things? Would he love me less?"

My alarm grew as I realized my best efforts were limited and imperfect. I may be talented at some things, but God is perfect. I may be intelligent, but God's knowledge and wisdom have no bounds. I may be helpful, but my efforts are puny compared to God's sacrificial love. If I couldn't impress God with my natural attributes, talents, or service, then I was unsure why God loved me. I felt troubled and began to search for a better answer for God's goodness.

Why does God waste his time caring for us? There is nothing we can do to earn his love and attention, yet he unreservedly pours his interest, concern, and compassion out on to us. It isn't because we deserve it. I definitely don't. He behaves compassionately, mercifully and lovingly because these actions express who he is rather than what we deserve. In other words, God's nature is good. A.W. Tozer puts it this way: "The goodness of God is that which disposes Him to be kind, cordial, benevolent, and full of good will toward men. He is tenderhearted and of quick sympathy, and His unfailing attitude toward all moral beings is open, frank, and friendly. By His nature He is inclined to bestow blessedness and He takes holy pleasure in the happiness of His people."[3] He goes on to explain that "Divine goodness, as one of God's attributes, is self-caused, infinite, perfect, and eternal. Since God is immutable, He never varies in the intensity of His loving-kindness. He has never been kinder than He now is, nor will He ever be less kind. He is no respecter of persons but makes His sun to shine on the evil as well as on the good, and sends His rain on the just and on the unjust. The cause of His goodness is in Himself; the recipients of His goodness are all His beneficiaries without merit and without recompense."[4]

Why does God behave the way that he does? Because he is good. We cannot compel him to act right; he does so because it reflects and expresses who he is. God's goodness may feel impersonal and undeserved since it is a part of his personality. Most of us work to be special to the ones we love. We go out of our way to earn their attention. But God's love cannot be won this way, and it has nothing to do with our worthiness. However, this is actually a blessing. God's innate quality of goodness allows us to be the broken people we actually are. You can be confident in knowing that, no matter what you do, God's goodness is available and unchanged.

Although I don't understand why God loves me, I am confident that he does. And even though I may wonder why he puts up with me, his faith and tender care for me is self-evident. My spiritual crisis has helped to free me from trying to earn what had always been mine—God's goodness and love.

- Do you live your life trying to earn God's love?

- What would change if you believed that God's goodness is unchangeable?

- How have you experienced God's goodness this week?

OPTIONAL READINGS

Genesis 50:18–20
Psalm 86
James 1:17–18

DAILY DISCIPLINE EXERCISE

Read Psalm 86 known as a *prayer of David*. It is believed that it wasn't written in response to any particular situation, but rather it was a prayer David frequently used for himself.

PRAYER

Dear God, your goodness is so beautiful and undeserved. Thank you for taking such tender care of me. I am grateful that your compassion is not dependent on me. You know what a frail, imperfect person I am; yet you continue to pour your love out on me. Thank you!

DAY 5

Loving

What, then, shall we say in response to these things? If God is for us, who can be against us? He who did not spare his own Son, but gave him up for us all—how will he not also, along with him, graciously give us all things?

Romans 8:31–32

The desire to be known by another and the subsequent fear of losing that relationship is at the core of our hearts. From birth we gaze into the eyes of our parents or caretakers and look for our sense of value. Trust grows as they consistently provide for our needs. Through these relationships, we learn we are worthy of being cared for and loved.

In his book, *The General Theory of Love,* Thomas Lewis discusses this miraculous effect. The mother's love and compassion are critically necessary not only for the child's psychological well-being but also for his physiological growth. When the relationship goes well, the baby's physiological system is well regulated. Heart rate, blood pressure, and hormone levels stay within normal parameters, encouraging growth. On the other hand, when psychological processes go awry, the bodily rhythms within the infant are negatively affected.[5] Lewis writes, "Love, and the lack of it, changes the young brain forever."[6] All of us have been created to need to be loved.

With this basic hardwiring, it is not surprising that our ideal relational quality is unconditional love. This kind of love says we are precious, and that we are chosen without regard for our personal qualities or for any action we might take. It cannot be earned, is undeserved, and does not need to be reciprocated. It says, "I love you just the way you are, no matter what."

Is this kind of love possible? We look for it everywhere—from parents, friends, children, and spouses. Researchers have wondered if our high rate of divorce is due to unrealistic expectations. Unlike previous generations, we want our mate to be more than a stable provider or childcare provider. We want to marry our best friend. Unconditional love, unfortunately, rarely occurs in its perfect form once we become adults. Yet, we continue to long and look for this kind of love.

I have seen clients do strange things to keep their spouses or lovers in a relationship. Some of us will change ourselves so that we don't displease or disappoint our loved one. We might hold back parts of ourselves since we fear they might reject or misunderstand us. We develop a secret life or mask parts of ourselves to avoid upsetting the relationship. We put up with being chronically unhappy or abused to avoid having to face being alone.

Is unconditional love possible? Yes! But I believe your desire for unconditional love is a God-given spiritual condition. When you look to other people for this kind of love, you are actually seeking God. And only God is capable of establishing and maintaining this type of relationship with you. The hard part is to learn to stop looking for it in our connections with each other and instead to turn to God. Right now, God is pursuing you to be his beloved. You were designed at the moment of your creation to be his. Although this relationship was damaged by sin, God has made a way back to himself through his son, Jesus. Even now God is waiting for you to see his love offerings and to come running back to him. You can find our heart's desire of unconditional love when you recognize it is only possible from God.

- Where have you looked for unconditional love?

- In which of your relationships can you show your true self?

- What is your reaction to the idea that unconditional love is a spiritual condition?

- What gets in the way of you spending time with God and showing him your true self?

OPTIONAL READINGS
Isaiah 49:14–16a
John 3:16–17
1 John 4:9–10

DAILY DISCIPLINE EXERCISE
Read John's challenging words in 1 John 4:7–13 which urges us to look at our actions as evidence of our belief in God's love.

PRAYER
Dear God, your love for me is outrageous. I am a mess. I frequently avoid you by choosing to do other things instead of spending time with you. Forgive me for ignoring you. Your patient love is undeserved.

Concluding Thoughts

Sing, Daughter Zion;
  shout aloud, O Israel!
Be glad and rejoice with all your heart,
  O Daughter of Jerusalem!
The Lord has taken away your punishment,
  he has turned back your enemy.
The Lord, the King of Israel, is with you;
  never again will you fear any harm.
On that day
  they will say to Jerusalem,
"Do not fear, Zion;
  do not let your hands hang limp.
The Lord your God is with you,
  he is mighty to save.
He will take great delight in you;
  he will quiet you with his love,
  he will rejoice over you with singing."
Zephaniah 3:14–17 (NIV, 1984)

Psychologists are aware that we often attribute human emotions and qualities to inanimate objects and animals. Cars and ships are often referred to as "she." Pet owners frequently describe their animals' behaviors in human terms. We assume our worldview is universal by humanizing inanimate object and the animal kingdom. We do the same thing to God.

As we wrap up this brief look at God's nature, you aren't wrong to assume that God is like us in that he is an emotional being. There are plenty of biblical examples of when he granted mercy and experienced love and anger. The Holy Spirit grieves, comforts, and intercedes. And the New Testament records instances when Jesus expressed fatigue, grief, anger, agony, and joy.

We make a grave error, however, when we assume that because God is an emotional being, his motivations are identical to our own. God is not like us. He is holy, is like no other being, is perfectly complete, and is sovereign. His infinite nature is unfathomable, and if we look at his behavior from our limited perspective, you will feel confused or disappointed. Even though God often doesn't behave as you expect he should, and not all his actions will be understandable or even explainable, he is good, trustworthy, and loving. When feeling confused about God or challenged by life's difficult circumstance, let's work to know God better and learn to be still and wait on him. After all, there is no one like God.

Chapter 2

When Life Doesn't Make Sense

Why, Lord, do you stand far off?
Why do you hide yourself in times of trouble?

Psalm 10:1

I met Abby about the time she was starting high school. She was a student member at my local church and involved with various school activities. Her integrity and trustworthiness quickly made her one of my favorite babysitters.

During her junior year, Abby had won a spot on the dance team in an upcoming school play. Her parents and relatives were proud of her hard work and accomplishments. While practicing the routine with her dance partners after school one afternoon, Abby suddenly collapsed with an asthma attack. Although diagnosed with this disease as a younger child, she hadn't had any problems with it during recent years. A young man with medical training who happened to be on the school grounds rushed to her side and administered CPR. Meanwhile a teacher dialed 911. Despite these efforts, no one was able to reverse her failing condition. By the time the paramedics had arrived, Abby was gone.

I heard the news of Abby's death early the next morning. I felt shocked. Her life was just starting. She had had dreams of becoming a forensic pathologist just like the character Dana Scully on the then-popular television show *The X-Files*. She was ambitious, motivated, and passionate about God. She loved to serve others. Questions plagued me. Why did God allow Abby to die? How could this untimely loss be a part of his plan?

Life didn't make sense.

Isn't life supposed to be fair? Don't we believe that those who commit evil acts should be punished while those who are good and serve others should be rewarded? But it rarely works this way. Unfortunately, suffering is a part of life. I have personally experienced it, and, as a psychologist, I frequently bear witness to it.

What is the purpose of pain, loss, and suffering? Sometimes, when we are in the midst of a difficult situation, there is no answer that satisfies our desire to understand what is happening to us. We feel raw. We are angry. We demand to know "why?" Are we weak for experiencing these emotions? Is it wrong to feel doubt? Or anger? Is it a sin to ask God for a reason?

God is not afraid of your intense emotional reactions. Like a parent, he longs to comfort you when you suffer. Take Jeremiah, for example. He obediently prophesied God's words to the Israelites. Pashhur, the priest, overheard him and had Jeremiah punished. Jeremiah was beaten and put in stocks. In the midst of his pain, Jeremiah called out to God and prayed, "Cursed be the day I was born! May the day my mother bore me not be blessed! Cursed be the man who brought my father the news, who made him very glad, saying, 'A child is born to you—a son!'" (Jeremiah 20:14–15). Ouch! Talk about being honest. God understands your despair. He doesn't want you to hide from him, especially when you are hurt and angry. Instead, he desires you to honestly approach him in the midst of your pain.

Why is there pain and suffering? This is a very difficult topic. In this chapter we will take a closer look at five reasons for suffering and pain. If you find yourself feeling overwhelmed by your current situation or by your pain, please reach out to a friend, local pastor, or a Christian counselor. It is not a sign of weakness to ask for help. In fact, research has shown that it takes great psychological strength to seek help. You may also want to do more reading on the subject. There are some excellent books which explore the topic further.

For Further Reading on Suffering

Elliot, Elisabeth. *Suffering is Never for Nothing*. B&H Books, 2019

Keller, Timothy. *Walking with God through Pain and Suffering*. Penguin Books, 2013.

Tada, Joni Eareckson. *A Place of Healing: Wrestling with the Mysteries of Suffering, Pain, and God's Sovereignty*. David C. Cook, 2010.

OPENING QUESTIONS

Recall a time when life didn't make sense. How did it affect your relationship with God?

What occurred in this situation that challenged your faith?

How did this difficulty change you and your relationship with God?

WEEKLY DISCIPLINE INTRODUCTION

Journaling is a helpful practice. It is different than composing a term paper in that it gives you the freedom to write about anything you want and allows you time to process your thoughts and reactions as you journal. It works best if you approach this practice by sitting in front of a blank word-processing screen or an empty piece of paper, and let yourself write whatever comes into your mind. It is helpful to remember that there is no right or wrong way to do this and that it is a private practice to be kept between you and God. Feel free to express yourself in any terms comfortable to you.

DAY 1

Consequences

I consider that our present sufferings are not worth comparing with the glory that will be revealed in us. For the creation waits in eager expectation for the children of God to be revealed. For the creation was subjected to frustration, not by its own choice, but by the will of the one who subjected it, in hope that the creation itself will be liberated from its bondage to decay and brought into the freedom and glory of the children of God.

We know that the whole creation has been groaning as in the pains of childbirth right up to the present time.

Romans 8:18–22

God has given each of us the amazing privilege of self-determination. We are constantly choosing whether to do right or wrong, and our choices have consequences, including the possibility of hurting ourselves and others. Judas' betrayal led to Jesus' capture and death (Matthew 26:47–50). The chief priests had been looking for an easy way to dispose of Jesus. Judas knew the chief priests' intent when he accepted the bribe but let his bitterness rule (Mark 14:1–10). Judas' decision led to Jesus' death and later to his own suicide. His free will had far-reaching consequences.

My actions personally affect others. This line of cause and effect is easy to see. Everyone, myself included, has made bad decisions. We lie, steal, cheat, and get even with others. We violate God's law for momentary satisfaction or brief experiences of pleasure. It is odd how we are surprised when there are consequences for our actions, how, for example, a careless word or action while on the job might result in being fire, how an extramarital affair could lead to divorce, and how texting while driving just might kill someone. God was very clear: sin has far-reaching consequences—sin hurts us by damaging or destroying our lives and our relationships with others and at the same time pulls us farther away from God.

It is not only our actions that affect us and cause us to suffer; we are also affected by others' behaviors. Sin is terribly unfair as it indiscriminately destroys the perpetrator and the victim. All of us are touched by the deeds of others. We might be a child of divorce, a victim of abuse, or some other type of casualty of sin. No one escapes the effects of another's bad action. I personally know this kind of pain. As a preschooler I was molested by a cousin. This occurred in the mid-1960's when sexual abuse was an awkward topic, and counseling opportunities and resources were limited. The effects were staggering. I struggled to fit in at school and had many odd fears. My family and I did not receive any therapy to help us process the trauma. I often wondered where God was, did he see my pain, and did I matter to him. I knew I had done nothing wrong and didn't deserve the psychological and social aftermath of the attack, yet I still suffered.

Each of us holds the power of self-determination. Exercising our free-will can have amazing results, like enabling us to run a 10k race, helping a friend in need, or resisting the urge to gossip when out with a friend at a local coffee shop. When used for ill, however, it comes at a terrible price: wounding ourselves and others. All of our actions have a ripple effect. The Bible warns us that our sin will have consequences that last until the third or fourth generation of our children, whereas our obedience will result in God showing love to a thousand generations (Exodus 20:5). What we sow, we will reap (2 Corinthians 9:6).

Although it is hard for us to understand, God continues to give you the freedom of choice because of his great love for you. Not only does this include the choice to do good or evil, but also whether or not to love and serve God. After all, it is your radically loving God himself who has the most to risk.

- When has another person's actions negatively affected you?

- Did it affect your relationship with God?

- Why do you think God continues to allow you free will, even when your actions may hurt others?

OPTIONAL READINGS

Matthew 5:43–48
Romans 12:9–21

DAILY DISCIPLINE EXERCISE

Use today's questions to write about a painful experience with another person. Is this an on-going issue? What did you learn about yourself? About God?

PRAYER

Dear God, there has been pain in my life due to sin. Some of it has been due to my bad choices, whereas some is a result of others' actions. I don't understand why you allow this to happen; yet I know you value my freedom of choice. Help me to trust your plan, especially when I am in pain.

DAY 2

Persecution

I have given them your word and the world has hated them, for they are not of the world any more than I am of the world. My prayer is not that you take them out of the world but that you protect them from the evil one.

John 17:14–15

I came across a story of an Iranian pastor, Behnam Irani, who was arrested in 2010 when government security officers stormed his house church service, interrogated attending members, and confiscated Christian materials.[1] He was assaulted and taken into custody on charges of apostasy. Found guilty, Pastor Irani was sentenced to serve a five-year term at Ghazal Hesar, a prison known for its inhumane treatment of prisoners. Early reports indicated that Pastor Irani had been beaten by fellow prisoners and was gravely ill. The family worried Pastor Irani would die without proper medical care. At the time I read this story, it was believed he was still alive and serving his sentence.

Jesus warned that because of our faith we would face all kinds of persecution. Pastor Irani knew the cost of his belief. He was arrested four years earlier for the same crime. Yet he continued to open his house and to pastor fellow seekers. He did not let the threat of suffering deter him from his service and devotion to Christ.

Since Jesus was despised by many people, we shouldn't be surprised when we encounter the same kind of rejection. In fact, Jesus' prayer, as recorded in John 17, warns us that we will be misunderstood and come under attack. Jesus himself regularly faced persecution. Pharisees often plotted to stop him and finally to kill him. Jesus told us we also should expect to be persecuted. "Blessed are you when people insult you, persecute you and falsely say all kinds of evil against you because of me. Rejoice and be glad, because great is your reward in heaven, for the same way they persecuted the prophets who were before you" (Matthew 5:11–12). The Bible is filled with examples of believers who suffered for their faith. Stephen was stoned for proclaiming the truth (Acts 7:54–60), Paul was imprisoned, flogged, and beaten (2 Corinthians 11:23–28), and seven of the original eleven disciples were martyred.

This kind of persecution continues today. Around the world, Christians like Pastor Behnam Irani are in prison for preaching the gospel of Christ. In some parts of the world, new believers are being rejected by family members when their conversion becomes public. Others have been tortured or killed simply because of their obedience to God.

The enemy of God hates Jesus Christ and all who do his work. Although many of us tend to be insulated from the most severe forms of persecution, you should not be surprised when you encounter the same kind of rejection and persecution. Finally, we need to remember to pray for our brothers and sisters in Christ who are right now facing rejection, suffering, and even death, for their faith.

- Have you ever come under attack for your Christian beliefs?

- What was your reaction?

- How did God help in that situation?

OPTIONAL READING

1 Peter 4:12–16

DAILY DISCIPLINE EXERCISE

Consider journaling about what comes to your mind when you think about the topic of spiritual persecution and how it personally relates to you.

PRAYER

Dear God, thank you for praying for my protection. You have warned me that I shouldn't be surprised when I come under attack for my faith. Strengthen and equip me to face such challenges. Protect me from discouragement when persecution happens. And please act on behalf of my fellow believers around the world who are facing persecution because of their faith in you.

For more information on the persecuted church, please visit: *http://www.persecution.org/* and *http://www.persecution.com/*

DAY 3

Maturity

...but we also glory in our sufferings, because we know that suffering produces perseverance; perseverance, character; and character, hope.
                                                                Romans 5:3–4

Military leaders know good soldiers are prepared for every possible contingency. They must be equipped to deal with sleep deprivation, hunger, inclement weather, and being under attack. This kind of readiness only comes when their men and women have been trained under stressful conditions.

Don't not be surprised when you face the same kind of conditioning. As Paul reminds us, we are soldiers of Jesus Christ (2 Timothy 2:3). Trials and difficult circumstances strengthen your faith. Pain forces you to examine our beliefs and to discard anything shallow or immature. You are urged to "consider it pure joy, my brothers and sisters, whenever you face trials of many kinds, because you know that the testing of your faith produces perseverance. Let perseverance finish its work so that you may be mature and complete, not lacking anything" (James 1:2–4).

I grew up singing hymns written and composed by Fanny Crosby. Fanny was blinded at a young age. She could have become an embittered, depressed person; instead, she wrote songs of joy and trust. One of my favorite songs of hers is "Blessed Assurance." The third stanza begins with these words: "Perfect submission, all is at rest! I in my Savior am happy and blest."[2] A preacher once told Fanny it was a pity God didn't return her sight. She responded that if she had been given the choice at birth, she would have asked for blindness.

When asked why, she replied, "Because, when I get to heaven, the first face that shall ever gladden my sight will be that of my Savior."[3]

James 1:2–4 warns you to *expect* trials. When you face painful circumstances you shouldn't be surprised, rather you should consider them "pure joy." Why? Because hardship offers you an opportunity to examine your motives for obeying God. It challenges the foundation of your faith. And when you choose to obey and persevere despite uncomfortable circumstances, your spiritual maturity grows. Like soldiers who are trained to face combat in unfamiliar and dangerous terrain, the testing of your faith equips you to do God's work more effectively. (Romans 5:3).

- Tell of a hardship that has tested your faith.

- How did this circumstance affect you spiritually?

- How can you become more like Fanny Crosby, who saw her disability as a blessing?

OPTIONAL READINGS
2 Timothy 2:3–5
Hebrews 12:1–3

DAILY DISCIPLINE EXERCISE
You might want to use today's questions as prompts to your journaling.

PRAYER

Dear God, you are clear in your word that trials will come. Please don't let me become bitter from such experiences. Make me more like Fanny Crosby. I want to trust you in all circumstances.

DAY 4

God's Glory

But we have this treasure in jars of clay to show that this all-surpassing power is from God and not from us. We are hard pressed on every side, but not crushed; perplexed, but not in despair; persecuted, but not abandoned; struck down, but not destroyed. We always carry around in our body the death of Jesus, so that the life of Jesus may also be revealed in our body. For we who are alive are always being given over to death for Jesus' sake, so that his life may also be revealed in our mortal body. So then, death is at work in us, but life is at work in you.

2 Corinthians 4:7–12

Paul had a physical problem he called a thorn. He asked God to heal him of it on three separate occasions. In fact, it is recorded that Paul "*pleaded*" (2 Corinthians 12:8) for God's intervention. The use of the word plead suggests that this physical affliction caused Paul great discomfort, personal hardship, and possibly suffering. Scripture records, however, that Paul's attitude shifted from "pleading" to "boasting" of this weakness in his letter to the Corinthian church. He said, "That is why, for Christ's sake, I delight in weaknesses, in insults, in hardships, in persecutions, in difficulties. For when I am weak, then I am strong" (2 Corinthians 12:10).

Paul learned a spiritual lesson that allowed him to embrace his condition. He discovered, in addition to it making him humble and dependent on God, his weakness brought glory to God. Pain draws attention to our need for God, and it forces us to depend on him. When we persist through suffering, we become a living testament of God's victory over sin and death. Paul called this a "treasure in jars of clay to show that this all-surpassing power is from God and not from us" (2 Corinthians 4:7).

During my teens, I witnessed this kind of victory in Dwight Adams, my pastor's son. In addition to being a passionate Christian, Dwight was also a handsome young man and a successful athlete. He played football for his college's team and regularly ran to stay fit.

While attending college in 1971, Dwight started to feel unusually tired. Medical tests revealed he had leukemia. Dwight didn't let this stop him even though his prospects were bleak. While receiving chemotherapy, he continued to run several miles a day to combat the side effects of his illness and medications. Despite relapsing three times, Dwight was able to finish his Bachelor's degree. He had started DePaul University's Doctoral Program in Philosophy when he received bad news: the leukemia had returned for the final time.

Dwight's illness often gave him opportunities to witness to others about his faith. During his frequent hospitalizations, his parents recalled how he enjoyed visiting the rooms of the other patients so that he could encourage them and their families. Once, while traveling alone to receive treatment, Dwight picked up a hitchhiker. He asked the young man if he could introduce him to his best friend—*Jesus Christ.* Just a few months later Dwight met his best friend, Jesus, when he died at the young age of 24.

I remember the power of Dwight's testimony and how it touched me. He had such a passion for God. Why didn't God heal him? This is a hard truth to accept; suffering often doesn't make sense, but it can become an opportunity for God to be glorified. I know Dwight's suffering wasn't in vain. Many people were moved by his devotion to God and some even became believers. Even today Dwight's testimony and passion for Christ continues to have an impact for God as it encourages me and others to trust God. Like Paul and Dwight, you may discover that when you are weak, your humble reliance and dependence on God for all your needs becomes a mysterious strength that glorifies him.

- Have you experienced a time when God was glorified through your personal struggle?

- What were others' reactions to your hardship?

- How did God meet you during this period?

OPTIONAL READINGS

John 9:1–3
2 Corinthians 12:7–10

DAILY DISCIPLINE EXERCISE

Consider using this statement for journaling: "Like Paul and Dwight, you may discover that when you are weak, your humble reliance and dependence on God for all your needs becomes a mysterious strength that glorifies him."

PRAYER

Dear God, thank you for warning me to expect suffering. Give me the strength to get through such times. Let me be a witness to others and encourage them to trust in you. Let my life and pain bring you glory.

DAY 5

Deliverance from Evil

Be alert and of sober mind. Your enemy the devil prowls around like a roaring lion looking for someone to devour. Resist him, standing firm in the faith, because you know that the family of believers throughout the world is undergoing the same kind of suffering.

1 Peter 5:7–9

Recently the occult has become wildly popular with television shows that feature real-life ghost hunters, fictional series about witches, vampires, and demon hunters, and full-length feature movies about the battle between good and evil. The more rational among us dismiss this fascination as hogwash. We wonder if demon possessions, as accounted in the church's history and even by some missionaries in third world countries, are real. With all our advancement in science, especially in the medical and psychiatric fields, we wonder if these reports aren't actually cases of people struggling with an undiagnosed physical or mental illness rather than real examples of demon possession. Most psychologists and psychiatrics would agree that demonic possession and oppression do not exist, and, therefore, they do not recognize them as real conditions.

Although scientists in the Western world may not recognize evil as an actual presence that exists in a form of spiritual being, the Bible clearly disagrees. Jesus said that he came to "heal the sick, raise the dead, cleanse those who have leprosy, [and] drive out demons" (Matthew 10:8). He urged his followers to pray for protection from the evil one and warned that the devil has come to snatch or disrupt God's work in people's hearts (Matthew 13:19; Mark 4:15; Luke 8:12). In fact, Jesus spent a great deal of his time and ministry aiding people who were suffering from demon possession. Everywhere he traveled he took compassion on the spiritually possessed and set them free from their spiritual bondage. Gregory Boyd in his book, *God at War*, points out that Jesus "treat(ed) them (the demon possessed) as though they are casualties of war. For, in his view, this is precisely what they are."[4]

Even though Jesus said that he came to usher in the kingdom of God (Luke 4:43) and to destroy the devil's work (1 John 3:8), did he really mean that those of us who live in this modern age would still need protection from evil spiritual beings in the form of demons or from the devil himself? And if we should expect and prepare for spiritual warfare, in what form will that battle manifest itself today? There may not be clear answers to these difficult questions, but we need to realize that we are in grave danger if we either see Satan as too powerful and become terrified to take action or disbelieve he exists and, in response, become ineffectual and complacent.

However, Jesus clearly warned his believers that we will face real persecution and urged us not to discount the presence and personality of evil. Paul, in his letter to the Ephesians, urged us to prepare for spiritual battle against the powers of darkness. He wrote, "put on the full armor of God, so that you can take your stand against the devil's schemes. For our struggle is not against flesh and blood, but against the rulers, against the authorities, against the powers of this dark world and against the spiritual forces of evil in the heavenly realm" (Ephesians 6:12–13). As Peter in today's verse reminds us, the enemy of your soul, the devil, roams the earth seeking those he can destroy. We must not be lulled into thinking that this threat is unreal. He is not the stuff of myths and fairytales but rather a thief who comes to steal, kill, and destroy us (John 10:10).

How have you previously thought about the devil? Has it changed?

- What experiences have shaped your opinion?

- What steps have you taken to protect yourself from evil?

OPTIONAL READINGS

Romans 8:31–39
Ephesians 6:10–18

DAILY DISCIPLINE EXERCISE

Jesus taught his disciples to pray "deliver us from evil." What comes to your mind when you consider his instructions?

PRAYER

Dear God, thank you for Jesus' work of setting spiritual prisoners free from the devil's bondage. Forgive me for not taking the real presence of evil more seriously. Help me to recognize all forms of evil and to resist the devil's work in my life. Keep me from temptation and protect me from evil. Thank you that nothing, including any spiritual forces, can separate me from your love.

Concluding Thoughts

As he went along, he saw a man blind from birth. His disciples asked him, "Rabbi, who sinned, this man or his parents, that he was born blind?" "Neither this man nor his parents sinned," said Jesus, "but this happened so that the works of God might be displayed in him."

John 9:1–3

Jesus and his disciples encountered a man who had been born blind. When they asked why this man was handicapped, Jesus responded it was to bring glory to God. What the disciples were really asking was, "Whose fault was it?" They wanted to make sense of what seemed meaningless or incomprehensible. So, they oversimplified the situation and wondered who had done something wrong: the blind man himself or his parents.

I suspect the blind man's suffering frightened the disciples. It reminded them that they were out of control of life. The only way they knew how to make it understandable was to look for a reason or to find fault. Don't you wonder the same thing? If life takes a sudden turn or something bad happens, don't you want to know why? Aren't we all guilty of making the same connection as Jesus' disciple, looking for someone to blame?

Unfortunately, suffering will always be a part of life while we are here on earth. Instead of blaming yourself and others, we should prepare for it. God often uses pain as a wake-up call. It can make you spiritually aware and mature. It draws your attention to God's ability to sustain you as your need for him comes into sharper focus. And it forces you to depend on him rather than on yourself.

One day all pain and suffering will come to an end (Revelation 21:4), but in the meantime you are to place your hope in God and rely on him for all your needs.

Chapter 3

Psychological Need for God

For I know my transgressions,
 and my sin is always before me.
Against you, you only, have I sinned
 and done what is evil in your sight;
so you are right in your verdict
 and justified when you judge.
Surely I was sinful at birth,
 sinful from the time my mother conceived me.
Yet you desired faithfulness even in the womb;
 you taught me wisdom in that secret place.

Psalm 51:3–6

After being Egyptian slaves for over four hundred years and waiting another forty years to enter the promised lands of Canaan, Israel was a nation without a leader. God had planned to be their ruler, but the people sought to imitate the countries around them. Despite God's warning of the consequences, the Israelites insisted, and Saul was anointed as their first king (1 Samuel 8–9). Israel's decision went horribly wrong. Not only did all God's dire predictions come true, but Israel eventually divided and its people were taken into captivity.

This, however, was not the first time God's ideal plan had been set aside. God gave humanity the incredible gifts of self-consciousness and self-determination. As he breathed into Adam the "breath of life" giving him a soul and a spirit, Adam became a "living being" (Genesis 2:7). And with that act, humanity was made self-aware and a free agent. Adam and Eve began to wrestle with existential questions, such as who will define their identity? What would give them self-worth? Would they remain faithful to God? How far will their dominion and authority extend? Can they accept their place in the hierarchy, knowing they are not equal with God, but rather his creation? Adam and Eve's thirst for knowledge of themselves and the world around them, however, led them to seek information outside of God's will and plan, causing sin to enter the world. This destructive act damaged the human heart, causing self-interest to be the paramount concern of Adam's offspring and set in motion a repeating pattern of God's offer of lordship and intimacy to be rejected.

Humanity's spiritual fall did more than damage our basic nature; it also led to spiritual and emotional isolation. Adam and Eve went from having spiritual intimacy with God to being cast out of the Garden of Eden. Their children never experienced such closeness with God but began their existence in sin and brokenness. What effects did their spiritual isolation have on their hearts and minds? How did it affect their sense of themselves and their interpersonal relationships? Jealousy, selfishness, and competitiveness were the new normal. Hatred and rage existed, and brother killed brother. In addition to spiritual separation from God, what if humanity's fall also stripped away the source of comfort and spiritual nurturance? Don't we regularly experience spiritual despair? Doesn't our spirit search for relief and comfort? With sin twisting and warping us, we suffer, distrust, and selfishly look first to ourselves. Like abandoned children, we lose hope and look to our own needs instead of turning to God.

What if we could become God-focused rather than egocentric, and compassionate rather than selfish? What if we could re-wind the clock and repair the damage sin has done to our psychological nature? The good news is that God has done just that by sending us his son, Jesus Christ. Just as sin entered into the world through Adam's defiant act (Romans 5:12), life and wholeness became possible through Christ's obedient death (Romans 5:17–19). Our broken and lonely hearts now have the opportunity to be truly healed. We can become who God intended us to be: fully alive—contented, accepted, valued, and with a sense of security and safety (John 10:10, Romans 8:37–39, Romans 15:13, Ephesians 2:5, Philippians 4:11).

In this chapter, through an integration of psychology and Biblical perspective, you will explore how God desires to be the author and shaper of your identity. Although the field of psychology in its pursuit to understand the development of the human personality has discounted God and the biblical perspective, truth cannot be denied or ignored, causing psychology to stumble into truth as it studies the human personality. This chapter will shift in its focus by weaving in more psychological theory as you explore your psychological need for God and God's intent to make you a whole and complete individual.

When loss or crisis strikes, we need to know that the ones we turn to for support, including God, are reliable and trustworthy. You will not meaningfully look to God during such times if you don't believe he understands you and is caring for your needs. In this chapter you will discover that God has an intimate knowledge of your basic psychological condition and is waiting to heal your broken spirits. Israel may have missed the incredible opportunity of being led by God as King, but you still have an opportunity to accept God's desire to be the definer and shaper of your self-image and personhood.

OPENING QUESTIONS

When you feel lonely, nervous, or overwhelmed, how do you comfort yourself?

Do you turn to God when feeling this way? If you do, describe what steps you take to find comfort in God. If you don't, why not?

Share with another person or journal about one of your spiritual concerns. Describe what you want to discover about yourself or God as this issue is addressed.

WEEKLY DISCIPLINE INTRODUCTION

Examen, or "examination of consciousness" is a beautiful spiritual practice described in Adele Ahlberg Calhoun's *Spiritual Disciplines Handbook*. She explains examen as a way of noticing how and where God shows up in our daily life. Through the use of questions, we examine our daily experiences in order to become aware of God's movement in the mundane activities of our life.[1] We observe nature around us, our interpersonal interactions, and the day's events for God's voice. We pay attention to the spiritual meaning of our reactions and feelings.

This week's daily spiritual practice will encourage you to pay close attention to your daily routines and to prayerfully ask God to show you what brings you joy, sadness, anger, and thankfulness. You may begin to notice how tuning into your psychological reactions and observations provides you another way to draw closer to God.

For more information on this spiritual discipline, please see Calhoun's book, *Spiritual Disciplines Handbook: Practices that Transform Us.* (2005).

DAY 1

God's Nearness

Where can I go from your Spirit?
  Where can I flee from your presence?
If I go up to the heavens, you are there;
  if I make my bed in the depths, you are there.
If I rise on the wings of the dawn,
  if I settle on the far side of the sea,
  even there your hand will guide me,
  your right hand will hold me fast.
If I say, "Surely the darkness will hide me
  and the light become night around me,"
  even the darkness will not be dark to you;
  the night will shine like the day,
  for darkness is as light to you.

Psalm 139:7–12

Psychological isolation is the most feared human condition. From the moment of conception it is essential that we connect to one another. This phenomenon was first observed in the early 1900's when babies who were housed in clean orphanage nurseries but with limited human contact had slow rates of growth and high rates of mortality. The identification of this condition, called "failure to thrive," led the field of medicine and psychology to understand that every person needs to be held, cuddled, and loved in order to reach his or her full physical and psychological potential.

One of my first clients had been diagnosed with failure to thrive as an infant. I began working with Kaley (not a real name) after she had been hospitalized where I worked on the child and adolescent psychiatric unit. As we walked down the corridor toward my office, I asked her what she wanted to do today. She shrugged, giving me her usual response. Walking behind Kaley, I noticed she was small. With her short stature, thin arms and legs, and tiny head, she looked to be about four years old instead of her chronological age of seven.

A few months earlier, Kaley had been removed from her home where she lived with her young mother and her current boyfriend. They often ignored her, forgetting to make meals for her, put her to bed, or get her to school. Truancy as well as subtle signs of abuse and neglect brought Kaley's situation to the attention of her elementary school teacher. Protective services temporarily removed Kaley from her home while her mother attended parenting skill classes and received counseling. Kaley wasn't settling well into her temporary foster home. The latest incident occurred when she attacked her foster mother after she insisted she go to bed.

Entering the room, Kaley turned off the lights, plunging my windowless office into complete darkness. I knew this game. Since our first counseling session several weeks earlier, Kaley started every appointment with her version of hide and seek. She never explained the rules to me since she rarely spoke. Instead, she flipped the light switch and disappeared into the blackness of my tiny room. There weren't many places to hide. My ten-by-twelve foot office was filled with a built-in desk, several bookshelves, and a chair, but Kaley would find some small corner.

"Where's Kaley?" I asked. I heard a giggle coming from the right side of the room, but acting like I hadn't heard her, I repeated the question. "Where's Kaley? Is she in here?"

I pretended to look for her, asking the same question. As I slowly got closer to the place where Kaley was hiding, her giggles sounded more excited. I suddenly swept in, tickled her, and pulled her into my arms as I proclaimed, "I found you!" She laughed and squirmed.

As the game ended, I turned on the overhead lights, looked back at Kaley, and said, "You thought you could hide from me, but I found you." A broad smile brightened her face. Kaley loved this game and especially loved this ending.

Kaley rushed back over to the light switch on the wall, turned off the lights, and started the game over again.

The years of neglect and abandonment had left Kaley with profound psychological questions. She wondered, "Do I matter?" "Am I alone?" "Can I be found?" Repetitively playing this game helped her to search for the answers to these troubling questions.

Don't we have the same concerns as Kaley? Don't we also wonder if God sees us? Don't we ask ourselves whether he knows we are alone and lost?

Kaley may have felt invisible and abandoned, but she was never hidden from me. She had nowhere to go; I only pretended to search and find her. Just like Kaley, you also are never hidden from God. The psalmist wrote, "Where can I go from your Spirit? . . . If I go to the heavens, you are there; If I make my bed in the depths, you are there" (Psalm 139:7a, 8). There is no place to hide from God's loving presence. He is always with you, searching for you, and calling out your name. He is waiting for you to hear him and to let his gentle arms pull you into his warm embrace.

 Tell of a time when you have felt the nearness of God's presence.

 What makes it difficult for you to believe God is near and waiting to rescue you?

- Is there an area of life where you need more of God and his presence?

- If you let God *find* you today, especially in those troubling areas, what might change for you?

OPTIONAL READINGS
Luke 15:1–7
Romans 8:38–39
Revelation 3:20

DAILY DISCIPLINE EXERCISE

Notice today when you feel emotionally close or distant from others. Do other physical or psychological states affect your connections to others? For instance, are you more vulnerable to feeling lonely or socially isolated when you are hungry or tired? When do you sense God? What does his nearness feel like? What conditions or circumstances affect or improve your awareness of his closeness?

PRAYER

Dear God, I may think I am all alone, but I never have been. Your Word tells me I cannot leave your presence. You go everywhere I go. I am not invisible or lost. If I feel alone, it is because I have not invited you into my situation. Please, Father, come find me. I need you today.

DAY 2

Psychological Security

My frame was not hidden from you
  when I was made in the secret place,
  when I was woven together in the depths of the earth.
Your eyes saw my unformed body;
  all the days ordained for me were written in your book
  before one of them came to be.
How precious to me are your thoughts, God!
  How vast is the sum of them!
Were I to count them,
  they would outnumber the grains of sand—
  when I awake, I am still with you.

Psalm 139:15–18

Each of us is built with an internal regulatory system that acts as our alarm system. Its purpose is self-preservation, and its desire is not only the protection of our physical well-being but also our sense of our *self* or our identity. It monitors for potential danger that would threaten the integrity of our identity. If we start to feel overwhelmed, misunderstood, invisible, lonely, scared, or stressed, this system kicks in and floods our body with the necessary hormones and chemicals to move us into action as we prepare to fight, flee, or survive by submitting to the outside pressure.

In the mid 1960's, Mary Ainsworth researched the types and strength of relationships between mothers (or primary care providers) and their babies. She devised a test, called the "Strange Situation," which had surprising results. Throughout the observation of the baby's reactions to a variety of situations, Ainsworth discovered four different "attachment styles" (or habitual ways of relating to others) and concluded the interpersonal fit of the mother-baby as well as the mother's parenting style had a profound effect on the infant's developing relationship style.[2] Ainsworth's ground-breaking study demonstrated that this protective regulatory system is immediately active at birth. Babies are born monitoring their environment's available emotional resources in order to protect their fragile developing identity. From birth, each of us is instinctually longing to belong and to feel safe, but we are on guard, defending our vulnerable sense of self. Early relationships shape what we later come to expect from others. If the world seems unsafe during early childhood, we anticipate insecurity and unavailability from others as we mature, but if our early childhood relationships are warm and accepting, we continue to expect such social ease during adulthood.

This discovery is not limited to our interpersonal relationships but also to our spiritual connection to God. Early wounds have a powerful effect on our ability to experience God's goodness and nearness since we use our early childhood emotional experiences to make assumptions about God and his availability. If others seem distant and cold, then we are more likely to believe God doesn't care and is uninvolved. However, if we have warm and fulfilling social relationships, then it becomes easier for us to experience God's love.

Although shaped by our first relationships, our attachment style continues to be influenced by others. Whether we are securely, anxiously, or ambivalently connected to others, we grow and change as we experience new relationships. This is great news since God is perfectly emotionally accessible. Because you are his design, he understands what threatens or delights you. He doesn't take over, overwhelm you, or leave you. It is his desire to completely fulfill you. You can find everything you need in him (Psalm 23:1). David, the psalmist, understood this very well. He wrote, "Keep me safe, my God, for in you I take refuge. I say to the Lord, 'You are my Lord; apart from you I have no good thing'" (Psalm 16:1–2). God sees you, knows you, and gently loves you. He is the safest *primary care provider* you could ever know, and waits to draw you close and to bring healing to your broken heart.

- Are you more likely to expect people to understand and support you? Or, are you more likely to worry that others will disappoint you?

- Do you find yourself making the same assumption about God?

- Since God perfectly cares for us, identify one area in your life where you would like to experience healing.

OPTIONAL READINGS

Psalm 3:1, 8
Proverbs 1:32–33

DAILY DISCIPLINE EXERCISE

How do you know when you are feeling emotionally secure? What does that sensation feel like? What does guardedness or danger feel like? In general, do you feel safe or insecure when you are around others? How about when you are spending time with God?

PRAYER

Dear God, thank you for being my perfect parent. Although your love, care, and support are readily available in all the right ways, I don't always have faith in you. Forgive me when I distrust you, and bring healing to my heart.

DAY 3

Self

Then the Lord God formed a man from the dust of the ground and breathed into his nostrils the breath of life, and the man became a living being.

The Lord God said, "It is not good for the man to be alone. I will make a helper suitable for him."

Genesis 2:7, 18

Introductory Note:

For the next three days of devotionals, we are going to observe a hypothetical baby's personality growth and development in order to understand several critical psychological challenges that occur. Let's pretend this child is female, but we will forgo naming her and instead refer to her as "our baby" or "our toddler."

At this point our baby is past the newborn stage, has found her hands, enjoys sitting up, is starting to crawl, and loves to chew on the toys within her grasp. She lives in a loving home with attentive parents. She knows she isn't alone in the world and finds her world to be safe and predictable.

As the first few months of life pass, our baby's budding personality begins to take more distinct shape and slowly she begins to realize she is her own person. At first it comes as a shock when she watches her loved ones leave the room. Feeling panicked, she tries crawling after the retreating figure of her parent. She sits in her crib and cries as she holds out her arms, hoping to be picked up. For the first time, she is aware that she is alone.

Previously, the awareness of her separateness was vague. Although her parents knew their identity was unique and separate from hers, her immature neurology at birth was not capable of this distinction. She only had a fuzzy sense of her self and instead believed that her primary caretakers were a part of her. However, at this stage of development our baby's rapidly growing brain begins to understand that mother and father are two different entities. This realization, however, comes in stages. Her first smile is met with delight as her parent responds with a grin. Cooing becomes a sweet game as adult and child imitate each other's behaviors. The world slowly becomes reachable as the infant discovers her hands. Sitting up and crawling add to her sense of independence. She realizes there are familiar and unfamiliar people giving rise to stranger anxiety. Our baby begins to understand that people can leave her alone, even if for just brief periods of time, causing separation anxiety to bloom. Coos change to simple sounds, then again to naming the important people and activities in her life. Each of these neurological advancements increases our baby's growing sense of self. She is just starting to discover she is her own person.

At about the age of two, our baby is becoming a demanding toddler who realizes she can limitedly manipulate her world. She feeds herself. She tries to dress herself. Demands of "me do it" become a frequent cry. Sharing is hard for her as she declares toys to be "mine." She now fully realizes that she is a unique person. Bath time, meals, or other daily activities become a battle as her growing personality attempts to maintain control over her own body. However, gross and fine motor skills are still immature, making manipulation of her environment difficult or awkward. Parents or other caretakers often have to help tie shoes, put on coats, brush teeth, and even wipe bottoms. Our toddler's fragile sense of identity often resists these aids. Tears of embarrassment or anger erupt as she tries to reject the help. Her lack of strength, however, means her will is often overridden.

Two polar opposite unconscious fears arise: engulfment and abandonment. Like the playground teeter-totter, these anxieties threaten to unbalance our toddler's developing identity and disturb her fragile sense of self.

Our toddler's first concern is abandonment, one of humanity's greatest fears. Unable to provide for her most basic needs, our girl unconsciously knows she cannot survive life on her own, so she avoids alienating the adults around her while working to preserve her own identity. She begins to balance her desire to exert her own will against her fear that she will frustrate others. She unconsciously worries she might be rejected and abandoned if she becomes too demanding. Like everyone else, she dreads being left totally on her own. Isolation is painful. So she tolerates, suppresses, and even denies some of her own desires in order to keep her loved ones emotionally close.

Engulfment is the opposite concern: the fear of being psychologically suffocated. This happens when our toddler, in an effort to avoid being abandoned by others, sometimes submits herself to the demands of others by relinquishing a part of her individuality. She unconsciously chooses to put aside her wishes in order to stay connected with her loved one. For example, she may not be a fan of orange juice, but to avoid being hurtful, she will drink Grandma's. She temporarily forgoes her personal preferences in lieu of maintaining important relationships. If appeasement becomes a constant requirement, such as having to do things repeatedly another person's way, then she will begin to feel as if she is being psychologically suffocated (or engulfed). It will begin to feel as if her sense of self is dying if she relinquishes too much or too often.

These concerns are not limited to the years of our toddlerhood. Abandonment and engulfment continue to exert pressure on our interpersonal connections and threaten our independence. Like a tightrope walker, we balance the need to live life on our terms against the need to be connected to others. Our twin desires for individuation (to be our own person on our own terms) and intimacy (being connected and having a sense of belonging with others) become a battle. When either spiral out of control, it is psychologically intolerable and potentially damaging to our developing psyche and interpersonal relationships.

In Genesis we see how God built into our hearts the desire to be our own person (independence) along with the need to be close with others (intimacy). In the creation story, it is apparent that Adam was different from the rest of the animal kingdom since he was a "living being" (Genesis 2:7). Adam was unique in that, just like God, he was completely his own person. Yet Adam also needed intimacy, so God created Eve. This was in addition to Adam's regular contact with God. Both relationships were important for Adam's psychological health. God understood Adam needed both: his own person yet also a part of community.

God understands you also fear abandonment and engulfment. He knows your identity cannot be completely formed unless these two fears are avoided, and he perfectly addresses these concerns. While allowing you to be fully yourself with all your preferences, tastes, and opinions, God never leaves you alone. He also is the perfect gentleman. Although he is infinite, omnipotent, and sovereign, he places so much value on your identity that he allows us to stumble around and make a mess of our lives.

- Describe an incidence of abandonment, either literal or emotional.

- Describe an occurrence of engulfment.

- Are you more likely to risk abandonment or engulfment?

- Have you ever worried whether or not God would take over your life and control you?

- Have you wondered whether God would reject and abandon you if you displeased him?

- How does it change your perspective to know God is a gentleman and respects your individuality?

OPTIONAL READINGS

Psalm 8:4–8
Acts 17:27–28

DAILY DISCIPLINE EXERCISE

Today notice how you stay connected to others while maintaining your personal preferences. Does your desire to be your own person ever feel uncomfortable? What is happening when this tension occurs? Do you ever forgo doing things your way in order to please another person's wishes and preferences? Does making this choice bother you? If so, why?

PRAYER

Dear God, you have created me to be uniquely and fully myself. You delight in my identity and understand its fragility. Thank you for being there for me while letting me be myself. Help me to relax in your presence and to share even more of myself with you.

DAY 4

True Value

*"Can a mother forget the baby at her breast
   and have no compassion on the child she has borne?
Though she may forget,
   I will not forget you!
See, I have engraved you on the palms of my hands;
   your walls are ever before me."*

Isaiah 49:15–16

Our growing toddler is now leaving the terrible twos and knows she is her own person. This is demonstrated in her preference for pink shoes, red barrettes, and chocolate milk before naps. She is getting better at dressing herself. She proudly helps by carrying her own plate and cup to the table. She may even be ready for potty training. The battle of wills is receding.

Our toddler is entering into a new psychological phase called developmental narcissism. She is now aware she is her own person with a separate identity from her mother and father, yet her sense of self, or identity, is fragile. She lacks confidence, is easily self-conscious, and is prone to shame. She wonders if others understand her and questions her level of importance to them.

Developmental narcissism was first noticed by a psychiatrist, Heinz Kohut, who was working in Chicago. Shortly after World War II, he noticed his patients were struggling with issues of low self-esteem and emotional insecurities. Through his work, he discovered every person has basic needs of empathic attunement (to be perfectly understood) and idealization (to be seen as special and unique to at least one other person).[3] Successful experiences of each nourishes our sense of self and helps us to become generous, confident, and healthy.

Empathic attunement is the emotional equivalent of looking at one's psychological self in the faces of our loved one. Just as we want to see our physical image in the reflected surface of a mirror, we need to feel that our emotional self is understood and interpersonally reflected back. This is called emotional attunement. It is the harmonious agreement between the one who is having the experience and the other who understands the exact tone and meaning of the experience. Just as musicians tune their instruments to each other before a concert, we look for others to modulate and resonate with the tone of our feelings.

The desire for emotional attunement can occur at any time but is most needed when something shakes our confidence. For example, our toddler falls down on the driveway. As she stands up, she sees her bloodied, scraped knee and rushes toward her mother, crying. Approaching her mother, she looks for signs on her mother's face that she is concerned. She wonders if her mother notices her pain, if her distress matters, and if her mother understands the depth of her need for comfort. The warm embrace and the soothing expressions of her mother's concern comfort her. Her abrasions are washed with a warm cloth and her injury is sprayed with a cool antiseptic. Her mother covers her wound with kisses as a Band-aid is applied. Even though her physical injury hasn't changed, her sense of pain diminishes. Her mother's successful efforts of attunement calm her and soothe her wounded ego.

Another basic human need of this developmental stage is idealization. We need to feel that we are extra-special to another person. We look to have our accomplishments applauded and our work admired. These individuals are often our adoring parents. Everything we do is "oohed" and "ahhed" over, and when we look at our parents' faces, we see their pleasure with us. When loved like this, we feel as if we are perfect, wonderful, and delightful. We enjoy knowing our parents only have eyes for us.

This psychological phase is important as we consolidate our growing sense of self. It teaches us that we matter, at least to one other person. Successful mastery of this stage allows us to take risks, such as competing in sports or music. We gain a healthy self-confidence and a sense of our own worth and value. We learn how to soothe and comfort ourselves and are able to develop stable interpersonal relationships.

This developmental phase is intentional. God purposefully designed you to need attunement and idealization. He knows you need to understand your value. We see God's awareness of this when he repeatedly rescued his people. He concealed Adam and Eve's nakedness and shame by covering them with animal skins (Genesis 3:21). He instructed Noah to build an ark with the exact dimension to withstand the terrible flood. He even shut its massive doors (Genesis 7:16). He sent angels to rescue Lot and his family from Sodom and Gomorrah (Genesis 19:15). God is so empathically attuned to your needs that he sent his only son to his death in order to save you from your sins (John 3:16). As evidence of his great love, God has "engraved us on the palms of his hands" (Isaiah 49:16) where it will be seen for all of eternity.

- Describe a time when you experienced emotional attunement. How did it feel? How did it affect you?

- How about a time when you felt idealized by another? How did that experience impact you?

- What Bible verses remind you God is attuned to your needs and idealizes you?

- How does knowing the depth of God's adoration for you affect you?

OPTIONAL READINGS
I Chronicles 4:9–10
Jeremiah 29:10–14

DAILY DISCIPLINE EXERCISE

Do you have someone in your life who observes and comments on your emotional state? Does this person notice when you are tired, stressed, or upset? How does this feel? If there currently isn't this kind of relationship in your life, how does it feel not to have this kind of emotional support?

PRAYER

Dear God, you are my perfect, adoring Father. You have withheld nothing to love and save me. Let the depth of your love touch me. Heal my heart where I doubt my worth to you. And help me to live more confidently as your beloved child.

DAY 5

Restoration

This righteousness is given through faith in Jesus Christ to all who believe. There is no difference between Jew and Gentile, for all have sinned and fall short of the glory of God, and all are justified freely by his grace through the redemption that came by Christ Jesus.

Romans 3:22–23

Are all desire good? If not, what makes them wrong or inappropriate? How do we tell the difference between an acceptable and selfish desire? What about feelings of guilt? What role does it play? Should we entertain and address internal incriminations? Then there are the demands of daily life. How does the pressure of managing our basic needs and other interpersonal relationships affect us? Such questions highlight the complexity and sophistication of our psychological self. It is adaptable, malleable, and multi-faceted, and at any given moment, many competing forces are at work. For instance, while sitting on the couch and relaxing, we may feel guilt and incrimination about unfinished chores. Feeling already too full, we are conflicted as we take the last bite of our dinner meal. A battle rages inside as we strive to feel happy, respected, and satiated. We want others' approval and to avoid social stigma and punishment, while simultaneously trying to please ourselves. Are these internal drives God-given? Should they always be expressed and trusted?

Sigmund Freud, a neurologist born in the late 1800's, noticed the complex forces that affect our decisions and actions. He speculated that there were three main competing drives that shapes all of human behavior: we have an innate desire for pleasure (which he called the "id"), a competing wish to avoid shameful or unpleasant experiences (or "superego"), and the challenge of addressing these needs (which he called this part of our self the "ego") while navigating the pressures of the real world. Each of us works cooperatively with or against these internal forces to get what we want.

Let's use our imaginary baby to understand these internal drives better. At birth, she wants instant gratification. She is unaware that her demands are unreasonable or selfish and doesn't care how she affects others since she doesn't have morals and lacks judgment. She is only deterred by experiences of pain and discomfort. She howls when she is wet, cold, or hungry, and demands her needs be met the moment she experiences them or feels the slightest twinge of distress. She doesn't know how to wait her turn and cannot be persuaded to be reasonable. In other words, she wants what she wants when she wants it.

However, relating to the world this way isn't very successful since reality often impedes or thwarts instant gratification. As a result, our baby begins to learn she must negotiate or navigate complicated situations or relationships in order to achieve her goals. She slowly learns to wait her turn as her desires and impulses become governed by wisdom, good judgment, and insight. And with practice, her ego begins to grow and develop as she copes with obstacles that delay or impede her desire for immediate gratification.

As our baby grows and moves through toddlerhood and into the preschool years, a new pressure appears: she wants to fit in. In an effort to be pleasing, she begins to monitor herself. This gives rise to the development of an inner critic within herself, which is an immature precursor of her conscience. It points out her faults and failures. Perfectionism becomes a new goal as she becomes aware of social norms. If she thinks she has behaved in socially unacceptable ways, she punishes herself with feelings of shame and judgment. Feelings of anxiety and guilt appear as she unconsciously worries about being rejected by others. Certain behaviors and thoughts now become taboo, particularly those previously disapproved by or punished by her parents. Her new goal is to be a good girl, and she internally monitors herself for threats to this objective.

Freud's observations spurred further speculations and observations about human personality development. Recent medical and neurological advancements have revealed an extremely sophisticated biological process that aids us to emotionally fit in with others. Although we have been made in the likeness of God (Genesis 1:26, Genesis 5:1, James 3:9), fearfully and wonderfully created (Psalm 139:14), and stand a little lower than our perfect, divine God (Psalm 8:5), our nature— including our desires, our intellect, our conscience, our emotional reactions, and our ability to determine the course of our daily life—have been corrupted by sin. We are born with a bent towards selfishness (Genesis 8:21) and are "deceitful above all things and beyond cure" (Jeremiah 17:9).

Although you cannot fix this, your condition is not beyond God's ability to redeem and restore. Rather than indulging in or denying yourself in the pursuit of self-improvement, you need to submit yourself to God who is able to transform you by renewing your mind (Romans 12:2). He purifies your hearts and cleanses your spirits (Psalm 51:7,10), and gives you the ability to discern his will so that you can determine what is "good and acceptable and perfect" (Romans 12:2).

- Do you find it hard to share the selfish or dark side of yourself with God? What makes it difficult?

- Do you believe and trust your desires or your sense of guilt? How does it change your perspective to know that every part of yourself is born sinful and broken?

- Do you find yourself trying to earn God's love by being good?

- What would change in your daily life if you trusted God for your goodness?

OPTIONAL READINGS
Psalm 51
Romans 6:12–23

DAILY DISCIPLINE EXERCISE
How do you know when you are good enough? What occurs within or around you when you feel that way? What would change if you stopped trying to save yourself, but instead relied on God's grace and his work in your life to heal you? How do you know when you are looking to him to save you instead of trying to earn your salvation?

PRAYER
Dear God, you completely know me. Nothing in me is hidden from you. I feel so ashamed of my sin and darkness. Please come into my mind and heart; and set me free from my brokenness. Wash me, cleanse my spirit, and renew my mind so that I can know and do your will.

Concluding Thoughts

"There is no one righteous, not even one;
 there is no one who understands;
 there is no one who seeks God.
All have turned away,
 they have together become worthless;
there is no one who does good,
 not even one."
"Their throats are open graves;
 their tongues practice deceit."
"The poison of vipers is on their lips."
"Their mouths are full of cursing and bitterness."
"Their feet are swift to shed blood;
 ruin and misery mark their ways,
and the way of peace they do not know."
 "There is no fear of God before their eyes."

Romans 3:10–18

God has designed you to be uniquely yourself. Just as there are no two fingerprints and DNA alike, your identity is also unique. Once born, your personality quickly takes shape as you begin to see yourself as separate from those around you. Being assured that you are psychologically safe allows you to explore. We need to know that others are near and care about us. Yet becoming your own person is paramount as you strive to find the balance between being independent while staying interpersonally connected.

Despite years of study, the field of psychology continues to debate the intricacies of this developing self. Counselors spend thousands of hours each year working to help suffering clients undo what has gone wrong during the critical developmental years. Although psychology attributes the causes of our emotional issues to early childhood difficulties, it is clear that sin has had a powerful impact on our fragile sense of self. We have been warped and twisted from God's original design. Thinking we can solve our problems and address our psychological pain on our own, we pursue self-interests instead of God's will. This only worsens our condition and leaves us with more scars on our delicate identity.

We need God. This reality becomes the clearest when pain and suffering strike. However, if God doesn't feel accessible or safe, we are at risk of trying to address our suffering through human efforts. It is not surprising that addictions, depression, anxiety, and other psychological difficulties often manifest when we cannot escape or make sense of pain.

God understands. You are fearfully and wonderfully made. He patiently waits for your invitation to let him into your hearts and to make you a new creation. He renews you, restores you, reassures you, and delights in you. He perfectly loves you and works to help you recover psychological wholeness.

Chapter 4

Comfort in God

"He will cover you with his feathers, and under his wings you will find refuge; his faithfulness will be your shield and rampart."

Psalm 91:4

Occasionally a client tells me about such painful circumstances that I am overwhelmed. I find myself struggling to be helpful. I wonder, "How are we supposed to cope with such inconceivable pain and injustice?" "What are we to do when we face misfortune?"

And then I think, "What should we expect from God during such times?"

Several years ago, a painful experience with my son provided me some new insight into these challenging questions. My middle son who was a toddler at the time developed asthma symptoms. I took his symptoms seriously and made an appointment with a specialist. She explained he needed to undergo allergy testing which consisted of two steps. The first procedure required him to lie still while dozens of tiny pins pressed into his back for a second. This went beautifully. He lay perfectly still, cooperating with the process while I let out a sigh of relief.

For the second step, a nurse had to inject seventeen intradural (just beneath the skin) injections up and down his upper arm. As the nurse came into the examination room with a tray full of tiny hypodermic needles, my son's eyes became wide with fear and he began to move toward the door. The nurse looked at me and asked for help. I brought him back, pinned his tiny body between my legs, and held down his flailing arms. He began to scream, each yell becoming louder with every injection.

My hands and legs began to tremble as I listened to his cries. I felt horrible. I knew this had to be done so that he could be diagnosed and treated. Tears rolled down my cheeks as I held on.

There was a pivotal moment during the procedure when my son looked up at me. His face was bright red, splotchy, and wet from crying. His eyes stared at me with a desperate intensity. With his accusing glare, I could see his unspoken question, "Why are you doing this to me?" "I trusted you!" In that moment I knew he believed that I had betrayed him, and my heart broke.

How do you explain to a three-year-old the reason for pain? Nothing I said would have made any sense to him. All he was capable of understanding was that I allowed his misery, yet I was really trying to save him. How many times has God had this same experience with us?

I have often wondered if our pain and suffering have a purpose. I wished my pain made more sense to me. I think understanding its reason would make it seem more bearable. Just as I could not explain the reason for the medical injections to my three-year-old son, is it possible that there are times when God cannot explain the reason for our misery in an understandable way?

I know that there is real personal evil in the world, ranging from small petty actions that prick us to terrible atrocities that threaten to destroy us. Some theologians believe that God is all-controlling and that everything that happens is part of his grand design, whereas others believe our God-given free will is truly free and includes an opportunity to bless or curse each other. However, my theological beliefs about God's sovereignty seem moot when I am suffering. Instead I wonder how will I survive when suffering strikes, and how will I hold on to my faith during trying times. And finally, I ask the question, "Will God take this difficult experience or circumstance and use it for his good?"

A friend of mine shared a story that exemplifies this tension. In the midst of an ugly divorce, my friend decided one evening to drive over to her soon-to-be ex-husband and his pregnant girlfriend's residence and confront them. Instead of giving them a piece of her mind, she found herself unexpectedly offering forgiveness. She left their apartment angry, shocked by her reaction, and dissatisfied. A year later she received a letter from her ex-husband's girlfriend who shared that the experience of being forgiven moved this young lady to dedicate her life to Christ. Instead of comforting my friend, this only angered her further. She began to wonder if God had deliberately put her through this terrible situation in order to save this one woman. Although some people might take comfort from this thought, my friend admitted that it left her feeling used. It was later when my friend came to the belief that God didn't orchestrate her husband's unfaithfulness and marriage breakup as an elaborate effort to save this woman's soul. She camed to the conclusion, however, that God used this terrible situation in the best possible way so that something good came out of it.

On this side of eternity, we will continue to debate and struggle to understand God's sovereignty. But we can take comfort in the fact that, although life is unpredictable and cruel, God is not. Just as a child trusts the arms of her father as he holds her during a violent thunderstorm, we need to believe in the promise of God's presence.

What does it actually mean to have a child-like faith? Or to believe in God and to lean on him? Surveys regarding religious belief often show a surprising number of the population who claim to believe in God, yet their daily lives look no different from those who report having no religious belief. We may intellectuallys believe God exists, yet we often lack a practical faith that supports us when life turns hard. The question during such times becomes how do you practice what you believe? In this chapter you will explore five constructive ways to live a faith-filled life with God. It isn't enough to *know* about God; we need a *real experience* of God in order to be able to face all of life's circumstances.

OPENING QUESTIONS

Have you experienced a difficulty that shook your trust in God?

What particular detail of the situation challenged your faith?

How did your feelings about God get resolved?

WEEKLY DISCIPLINE INTRODUCTION

Meditation scripturarum is a meditation practice that uses a particular set of Scripture passages for contemplation. Literally translated, the word meditation means to think deeply. This spiritual discipline encourages us to ponder, reflect, and focus on God's word and the person of Christ. This practice is similar to *lectio divina* in that it uses a particular set of Bible passages; however, insight is gained by focusing on the content and context of the verses rather than looking for key words or verses that stand out. It helps to use your imagination and to visualize yourself in the setting. Also asking questions may deepen your understanding, such as who was the author, what was historically happening when this set of passages was written, and what situations were the verses addressing. Finally use what you have learned by applying it to yourself by questioning when have you felt this way and what situations were you facing. You may find that through this use of meditation practice God's word becomes alive and personal.

DAY 1

First Love

"I know your deeds and toil and perseverance, and that you cannot tolerate evil men, and you put to the test those who call themselves apostles, and they are not, and you found them to be false; and you have perseverance and have endured for My name's sake, and have not grown weary. But I have this against you that you have left your first love."
Revelation 2:2–4 (New American Standard Bible)

I remember my first love. I was ten and just started attending a new church with my parents. Sitting in the back pew observing the new pastor and the fellow churchgoers, I spied a tall, slender, older boy. I noticed his cute freckles and how his eyes sparkled with excitement and energy. It was then that I knew I was in love.

I followed him and his interests for over four years. Because we didn't attend the same school, I didn't mind going to church services three times a week since I knew he would be there. I tried to be in the general vicinity of him and became his invisible ghost. I loved everything about him; his laugh, his musical talent, and his mannerisms. He was my first crush, my first love.

My fascination ended abruptly when, four years later, I had my first opportunity to attend the same high school as him. Sharing a lunch period gave me an opportunity to know him better as I often sat and ate with him and his friends. I made a shocking discovery; we didn't have much in common. I found his competitiveness off-putting. He was too energetic and busy, and what I once found endearing about him was now irritating. It was then that I realized I never really knew him but had only loved who I thought I knew—an imaginary person.

Although there are many different kinds and qualities of love, such as feeling compassion, having affection, feeling fondly, or desiring another, we can't truly love (accept and value) someone we don't know, and we can't know someone unless we spend time—a lot of time—with him or her. This isn't just true for our social relationships; this is also true about our spiritual relationship with God. In today's Bible passage, John was writing to the church in Ephesus (Revelation 2:1–7). He started off by listing their wonderful deeds and faithful qualities. From the outside they seemed godly, yet God was no longer their first love.

What does it mean to have God as our first love? Jesus put it this way: he urged us to "love the Lord your God with all your heart and with all your soul and with all your mind" (Matthew 22:36). In other words, God is to be first in our heart and the focus of all our thoughts and actions. Since this statement sounds grand and lofty, the challenge becomes how do we practice it in our day-to-day life? I believe we are to take our cues from those who have recently fallen in love or from the love and bond new parents have with their infant. In both cases the loved person becomes an intense focus and top priority. All else becomes secondary. Everyday activities and interests shift and change as they are weighed against the impact of the primary relationship. New practices occur as some old habits are discontinued. Every other relationship, priority, and activity is assessed regarding its potential impact on this new relationship. Anything that distracts or negatively affects the primary love relationship is discarded. It is this kind of relationship God wants to have with us, and for us to have with him.

This kind of love is easy when it is new and exciting, but how do we maintain it for days, months, and years? As we read in today's verse, the church at Ephesus was having this problem. Obviously they had been faithful believers since they had a consistent religious practice, but something changed their heart's focus and passion for God. Outwardly they still appeared faithful, but inwardly they had replaced

God with other things. We must be on the alert for a similar type of falling away from God. If we are not careful, everyday pressures and stresses can and will slowly pull us away from our focus on God. However, we can find the answer to this problem in Jesus' example. Despite the intense demand on his time and for his attention, Jesus made it a regular practice to spend time with God. He frequently withdrew to pray and talk to God. God was always at the center of his thoughts, and he always put his relationship with his Father first.

God wants to be your first love. This is a huge demand, but it comes with unbelievable benefits. Besides eternal salvation (an amazing gift), everything else in your life will fall into place, despite your circumstances. Suffering and pain may be our companions here on earth, but making your relationship with God a top priority can bring us unexpected joy and peace.

Note:

This chapter's daily devotionals include an additional component called ***Practical Exercises***. Although each day offers three choices, choose the **one** that interests you the most or addresses a particular area of struggle.

PRACTICAL EXERCISES

1. Remember a time when someone became the focus or priority of your life. What changes occurred? How did your priorities shift? As time passed how did you sustain this passion? Have you ever felt this way for God (or Jesus)? Why or why not? How would your day-to-day life change if you made God this kind of focus?

2. Assess your faith practices. How often you do you read the Bible or pray? Do you practice other spiritual disciplines, such as gathering with fellow believers, fasting, meditating, and

worshiping? Prayerfully ask God what changes he would like you to make in regard to these habits. Maybe he wants you to become more consistent in one area, or maybe he would like you to add a new discipline. Be careful and make only one small, incremental change to your current habits rather than one large change or multiple changes.

3. Jesus took direction from God for every decision and interaction. We should too. In your current interpersonal relationships, focus on God's will and goal (vertical relationship) rather than your desired wishes and goals with the other person (horizontal relationship). Despite what happens or doesn't happen horizontally with others, work to please God with your interactions. To help with this exercise, ask yourself what God wants you to say or do in regard to your interpersonal matters. You may find yourself feeling calmer and less impulsive when dealing with relationship conflicts and challenges.

OPTIONAL READINGS
Deuteronomy 6:1–8
Mark 12:28–34

OPTIONAL READINGS
Read Psalm 37:1–11, 23–24. David was an older man when he wrote Psalm 37. At the time he penned these words, he had experienced great victories, terrible losses, and personal failure, yet he clung to God. How is God using David's wisdom about life and God's faithfulness to speak to you?

PRAYER
Dear God, forgive me for losing my first love for you. I am weak and fickle. I get distracted and behave selfishly. Please fuel my love for you. Help me to make you the center of my heart and of my life.

DAY 2

Trust

Humble yourselves, therefore, under God's mighty hand, that he may lift you up in due time. Cast all your anxiety on him because he cares for you.

1 Peter 5:6–7

Have you ever had the privilege of holding a newborn baby? She is so vulnerable. Her coordination is poor, causing her little arms and legs to tremble and wobble if she is not securely held. She blinks and looks at the world blurry-eyed since her eyesight is limited to the distance of eight inches. Everything is new, blindingly bright, loud, and chaotic to her. Nothing makes much sense. She hasn't acquired an understanding of language, shapes, or how to interpret the meaning of things. In addition to finding the environment around her confusing, she is also completely helpless. She cannot turn over, feed herself, or communicate a single need outside of crying.

At birth we must discover whether or not we can trust the world to successfully meet our needs. Erik Erikson, developmental psychologist, called this crisis the challenge of "trust versus mistrust." Being unable to care for ourselves, we, as newborns, are completely dependent on our parents. If we experience consistent care through regular feedings, physical provisions, and loving affection, then we discover that the world is dependable and trustworthy. We learn it is safe to rely on others and come to expect predictability and dependability from our environment. However, if our parents are inconsistent and unreliable in their care for us, we then become suspicious, withdrawn, and distrustful of others. And, instead of viewing the world as safe, we experience it is undependable, unpredictable, and dangerous.

Once trust is established with our primary caretakers, we will take unusual risks based on our internal assumption that our parents don't intend us harm. An interesting research study demonstrated the strength of this bond of trust between infants and parents. Babies were placed on a Plexiglas countertop, which had a steep visual drop off, and were urged to crawl across despite the apparent risk. Although there was no real danger due to the safety of the Plexiglas, the infants' visual immaturity and lack of experience lead them to be unsure. Faced with the situation of crossing over the visual cliff, the babies would look at their mothers, particularly their facial expressions, to gauge the riskiness of the situation. If their mothers were smiling and seemed at ease, the children intuitively knew they were safe and were able to confidently cross over the visual abyss.[1] The mastery of the "trust versus mistrust" developmental hurdle enabled the infants to successfully face a potentially dangerous situation and to know that there was no real threat.

Just as we are extremely vulnerable and fragile at infancy, each of us also begins as spiritual newborns (2 Peter 2:2). Each of us also must discover whether or not we believe God is trustworthy. We desperately need God's provision and care, and, at some point, we will face a crisis that will drive home our state of utter helplessness. When this occurs, we become desperate and realize we are helpless. Our neediness creates an opportunity for us to seek out God as we discover we are spiritually destitute, and that without God's immediate intervention we are doomed. It was this type of desperation that Jesus was referring to when he told the listening crowd "blessed are the poor in spirit, for theirs is the kingdom of heaven" (Matthew 5:3).

It is only when we reach such a desperate place within ourselves that we discover God is trustworthy. We learn that we are not alone and that he has always been there, waiting for us to turn to him for help (Revelation 3:20). And as you reach out to him for help, you find that God is present, involved, and invested in your well being. Just like the infants in the research project who faced the test of a visual cliff, we can know that no matter how overwhelming or frightening our situation seems, God is with us and is keeping us safe.

This discovery strengthens your faith and spiritually matures you. It helps to prepare you to trust God with more of yourself, and it encourages you to turn to him quicker so that one day you will turn to him for everything.

PRACTICAL EXERCISES

1. Identify one area of your life where you experience stress or worry. Either write it down or share it with another person. Outline how you wished God would act in this area letting your ideas range from the practical to the wildly optimistic. Present your request and suggestions to God and continue to pray regularly about this matter. Notice how God is using Bible verses to speak you about this issue. What are your Christian friends' counsel regarding this issue? What does your conscience say? Ask God to make the answer evidently clear.

2. If worrying or fretting is an occasional problem, identify one common, repeating negative thought or worry. Write it down. When does this issue come up? How have you tried to address it? How successful has this effort been? Often we get into a habit of worrying about things that we can't change or have no control over. In fact, many of our worries are not solvable. Test yours to see if it has a solution. Ask yourself this simple question, "Is there an easy and reasonable solution to this concern?" If the answer is yes, then your issue is a practical problem that needs solving rather than a worry. However, if you are unable to answer this question quickly

and easily, then you are experiencing anxious thinking. Each time you discover yourself worrying; replace the anxious thought with another type of activity to distract yourself. Try creating a list of helpful distractions and use them each time you start to worry. At first you may feel like you having to do this process very often, but with regular practice you will discover that you are worrying less often and for shorter periods of time.

3. Remember one of your first efforts of reaching out to God and discovering his nearness. What circumstance or situation drove you to ask for his help? How did he reveal his love for you? What new thing did you learn about God's trustworthiness? Share that story with someone and remind yourself of this incident the next time you must trust God with something difficult..

OPTIONAL READINGS
Psalm 9:6–10
Psalm 31
1 Peter 2:2–3

DAILY DISCIPLINE EXERCISE

Read Psalm 31:9–20. David was on the run from King Saul. He had just narrowly escaped capture and was hiding in a cave. Despite experiencing persecution, betrayal, and hard losses, David's trust in God never wavered. He saw God as his deliverer and only hope. Are you being like David and relying on God? What issue or circumstances does God want you to entrust to him?

PRAYER

Dear God, I struggle trusting you. I don't turn to you quickly enough or often enough. Help me to recognize when I am relying on myself rather for you. I want to learn to trust you with everything, from the issues that keep me awake at night to the small mundane things. Thank you for always being there for me.

DAY 3

Surrendered Life

Some time later God tested Abraham. He said to him, "Abraham!"

"Here I am," he replied.

Then God said, "Take your son, your only son, whom you love—Isaac—and go to the region of Moriah. Sacrifice him there as a burnt offering on a mountain I will show you."

Genesis 26:2–6

It isn't enough to pursue God with our whole hearts, or to trust him when we get into sticky situations; we also need to obey him no matter how much it costs us. Abraham lived such a life. He followed God into a strange country, heard and trusted that he would be the father of a nation despite his elderly age, and then willingly went to the top of mountain with plans to sacrifice his much-longed-for child out of obedience. Why would God promise offspring to Abraham only to take his child away? It is because God would not accept being second best in Abraham's life. He wanted Abraham's complete surrender to his will and knew that Isaac posed a serious threat. So he forced Abraham to make a choice: save Isaac and disobey God, or obey God and lose Isaac.

It must have been an agonizing decision. I wonder if Abraham negotiated with God all the way to the mountaintop. Did he beg and plead? Was he confused and hurt? Did he wonder why God demanded what was most dear to him? A.W. Tozer, in his book *The Pursuit of God*, pointed out that Isaac was the living vessel or hope of God's promises to Abraham. He wrote, "Abraham was old when Isaac was born, old enough to have been his grandfather, and the child became at once the delight and idol of his heart. From the moment he first stooped to take the tiny form awkwardly in his arms, he was an eager love slave of his son…the baby represented everything sacred to his father's heart: the promises of God, the covenants, the hopes of the years and the long messianic dream."[2] Clearly God wanted nothing to stand in the way of him being the center of Abraham's life.

And just like Abraham, we are to live a surrendered life: one that is sold out and completely submitted to God and his will. Why do we find this so hard? After all, we intellectually know God is omnipotent, omniscient, and omnipresent. He is our creator (Genesis 1:1) and the lover of our soul (John 3:16). He knitted us to together (Psalm 139:13), longs to care for us (Psalm 23:1), and holds our future in his hands (1 Thessalonians 4:13–18). Although most of us say we trust God, it is when we are faced with a difficult dilemma or are challenged by painful circumstances that we see evidence of our doubt and disbelief. It is then that our rebellious nature rears up and demands we have things our way. Our sinful bent nature causes us to rebel and substitute our will for God's. We do not allow him to sit on the throne of our hearts; instead we occupy that place, and, at a deep psychological level, we innately disbelieve that anyone, including God, truly knows us or has our best interest. Instead, we selfishly believe we know better (Genesis 4:3–6; 2 Kings 5:1–15), want things done only our way (1 Samuel 15:17–20), have different priorities than God (Matthew 19:16–24, Acts 5:1–6), and often believe God's requests are unreasonable (Jonah 1:1–3).

Unfortunately, whether we recognize it or not, living life on our own terms will always lead to our destruction. Tozer writes, "There can be no doubt that this possessive clinging to things is one of the most harmful habits in the life. Because it is natural, it is rarely recognized for the evil that it is. But its outworkings are tragic. We are often hindered from giving up our treasures to the Lord out of fear for their safety. This is especially true when those treasures are loved relatives and friends. But we need have no such fears. Our Lord came not to destroy but to save. Everything is safe which we commit to Him and nothing is really safe which is not so committed."[3] Although, it may go against our nature and against logic and reason, we are called to die to our self and to our will. Jesus said, "For whoever wants to save their life will lose it, but whoever loses their life for me will find it" (Matthew 16:25).

God intimately knows you. He longs for you to be fully conformed to the image of Christ (Romans 8:28–30), and you can only have a truly satisfied life (John 10:10) when you completely surrendered to the will of God. Abraham may have occasionally stumbled in his spiritual life, but he made God the Lord of his life and obediently followed him, even all the way to the top of that terrible mountaintop with his son. His amazing faithfulness to God's will has never been forgotten, and God richly rewarded for him for living a surrendered life.

PRACTICAL EXERCISES

1. Identify one area in your life where you believe God is asking for greater obedience. How well are you doing with this? Define in practical steps what obedience looks like. At what point or step are you in the process? Is anything getting in the way of you following God's will for your life? If so, what is/are the obstacle(s)? Ask God to help you overcome the obstacle(s). You might find having the encouragement of an accountability partner or members of a small group helpful to you as you work to grow in this area.

2. Which of these four obstacles (believe we know better, want things done our way, find our priorities at odds with God, and/or sometimes believe God's requests are unreasonable) most often

gets the way of your complete obedience? Think of a time when this obstacle interfered with obeying. How did you resolve it? How is it causing problems in your spiritual life now? What did you learn from your past experience with this obstacle that might aid you with this situation?

3. Having an accountability partner can be a very useful relationship since it offers an opportunity to look at yourself and at your issues more honestly. Do you have such a person in your life right now? If so, how is it going? What has been helpful about that relationship, and how could it be improved? Periodically it might be beneficial to discuss the strengths and weaknesses of this relationship. If you don't have an accountability partner in your life, prayerfully look for someone God might be placing in your life who might be interested in assuming that role with you.

OPTIONAL READINGS

1 Samuel 15:17–23
Matthew 19:16–28

DAILY DISCIPLINE EXERCISE

Read Psalm 119:33–48. This set of passages is just two sections of twenty-two stanzas found in the longest psalm. Each set of eight verses represents one of the twenty-two letters in the Hebrew alphabet. Like a teacher, the author is giving instructions on the importance and value of God's law for our lives. How is God using these verses to remind you about the benefits of obedience?

PRAYER

Dear God, you have demanded my complete obedience to your will. You know that this is a very hard request. I often find myself distrusting you and pursing my self-interests. Please point out to me how perfectly you care for me and help me with my disbelief. Make me more like Jesus who was completely surrendered to your will.

DAY 4

Abiding

He gives strength to the weary
 and increases the power of the weak.
Even youths grow tired and weary,
 and young men stumble and fall;
but those who hope in the Lord
 will renew their strength.
They will soar on wings like eagles;
 they will run and not grow weary,
 they will walk and not be faint.

Isaiah 40:29–31

I looked at over Cathy who was next to me in the waiting room's tiny corridor. She sat tall in her chair, with her back rigid. Her eyes were staring forward and her hands were clasped in her lap. Every so often she would glance over at me and whisper, "Please pray."

The previous morning as Cathy finished spraying her hair and putting on the last touches of her make-up, she suddenly felt light-headed and lost most of her vision in her right eye. Over the past year, this medical condition had been occurring off and on for brief periods of time. This time it was different. Forty-eight hours later, her vision still had not returned. Now she waited in the tiny room for a medical technician to come and get her for further testing.

We live in a fallen, hurting world where things go terribly wrong. Mothers with young families should not lose their sight, children should not go to bed at night hungry, nor should any of us experience grief, loss, or pain, but we do. We live in a hard world that is "frustrated" and in "bondage to decay" (Romans 8:20, 21) which waits to be set free from the effects of sin. We intuitively know something here is wrong.

We sense we have been meant for more and yearn for things to be different. Deep within our hearts we long to find a place of paradise where we can live for forever in perfect peace and harmony with each other. Somehow we know we were meant to live in the Garden, not where we find ourselves: in a broken-down, cruel world.

This yearning for paradise drives us. I see it in every client I counsel. We work too hard, take on too much, overeat and drink too much, party too hard, or have indiscriminate sex. We buy bigger houses and nicer cars, work to keep our aging body looking young, and try to help our children get ahead. We are an anxious, exhausted, and unhappy people who search for a paradise that has been lost.

Jesus understood our internal fretfulness. He saw our striving and felt compassion. He knew this sin-filled world was never meant to be our home and urged us to abide in him. He said, "Come to me, all you who are weary and burdened, and I will give you rest" (Matthew 11:28). John, the author of five books in the New Testament, used the word "abide" over fifty times in his writings. The Greek word of *meno* means "to remain in place, to tarry, or to wait." It is a state of being rather than doing, yet it is given as a command. Jesus instructed his disciples to "remain in me, as I also remain in you" (John 15:4). He urged his followers to stay in his love, his word, and to remain obedient to his father's will. By abiding in Christ we are promised a productive life that bears fruit (John 15:5), and are warned that apart from Christ, all that we do is meaningless and unproductive (John 15:5–6).

Abiding is hard. It goes against our grain. We like to make something happen, often working at a problem until we find a solution. Abiding emphasizes our helplessness. It requires us to look outside our self for aid and support. We feel weak and useless, like we are not doing enough when we rest or *remain* in Christ. Maybe this is exactly the point. Learning to abide drives home our dependence and need for God. We are to look to him for everything, and nothing we do outside of his help will have any lasting consequences.

God knows you need him, and he eagerly waits to love you, to support you, and to give you rest. When you abide, you have real hope. This is not to be confused with the vague, fuzzy feelings of wishing everything works out well, but rather it is real assurance or a guarantee that God is with you and working all things out for your good (Romans 8:28). Abiding means you wait and rest on the expectation that God will fulfill all his promises.

It has been over two weeks since Cathy lost vision in her one eye. After seeing the best specialists, she still doesn't know if her eyesight will ever return. Although her life may be irreversibly changed, one thing remains the same; she is not alone as she abides in Christ. By leaning on him, she experiences his supernatural provisions. He promises to lend her strength, encouragement, and support, and he will never leave her side. It won't be easy for Cathy, but God will sustain her and help her to face the future with real hope.

PRACTICAL EXERCISES

1. As you consider your current lifestyle, where are you working the hardest? What is driving you? Listen to your feelings and analyze your concerns regarding this issue or area of your life. Is there any anxiousness or worry present? Have you prayed about this area? Are you trusting God for help and support? If not, why not? Begin to pray daily and ask for God's intervention and his will in this arena of your life.

2. What does the word *abide* mean to you? Remember a time when you *waited on God* and *remained in him*. What was different about

keeps you from trusting him and ask him to reveal himself more clearly to you so that your faith is strengthened.

3. Are you undergoing a particularly difficult time? If so, it might be especially hard to experience God's presence. Even when it doesn't seem to be true, God is with you. Discouragement and pain can make it hard to see where God is working in your life. Prayerfully ask God to make his presence known to you in a supernatural way, then, be on the lookout for evidence of his love. Be careful not to dismiss the kindness of others or other simple pleasures as proof of God's intervention and love.

OPTIONAL READINGS

Psalm 46:1–3, 10
Matthew 11:28–30
John 15:1–8

DAILY DISCIPLINE EXERCISE

Read Psalm 46. The author and historical setting of this psalm are unknown; however its content suggests some great calamity or national crisis was occurring. It is often referred to as *Luther's Psalm* since Martin Luther was known to sing the words of it during difficult periods. What crisis are you experiencing? How is God sustaining you through it?

PRAYER

Dear God, you promised to give me rest and strength to face life. I often forget and work too hard at trying to fix things by myself. I hate feeling out of control and helpless, which makes me feel weak. Please remind me that I am never alone. Help me to wait on you for all my needs.

DAY 5

Expectant Hope

The Spirit of the Sovereign Lord is on me,
  because the Lord has anointed me
  to proclaim good news to the poor.
He has sent me to bind up the brokenhearted,
  to proclaim freedom for the captives
  to release from darkness for the prisoners,
to proclaim the year of the Lord's favor
  and the day of vengeance of our God,
to comfort all who mourn,
  and provide for those who grieve in Zion—
to bestow on them a crown of beauty
  instead of ashes,
the oil of joy
  instead of mourning,
and a garment of praise
  instead of a spirit of despair.

Isaiah 61:1–3

Laura, my friend's teenage daughter, glided into the room with her new sequined dress recently purchased for the upcoming Swirl dance. Sliding her feet into her new glittering sandals, Laura hopped up onto a chair so that I could measure and hem her gown. Once I had finished pinning the hem, her mother and I watched Laura walk around the room, testing out the dress's new length. This was Laura's first official dance, and she and her mother were bubbling with excitement. Next on their list was to schedule a hair and manicure appointment. After hanging up the phone with the stylist, her mother looked at me, her eyes shining with pride for her daughter, and teasingly asked if I was glad I only had boys since it meant that I didn't have to contend with all the work of dresses, manicures, hairdos, and makeup. My heart froze, and I excused myself so that I could escape into a hidden hallway as the tears started to fall.

My friend had unwittingly opened an old wound of mine. Growing up with just sisters, I imagined one day I would have daughters of my own. I dreamed of making cookies, sewing doll dresses, and having tea parties with my girls. I couldn't wait to French-braid their freshly washed hair, to teach them how to knit, and to hold them tightly as they cried over the breakup of their first dating relationship. All these thoughts went through my head as I silently cried for the loss of my much longed-for imaginary daughters.

I think there is something special about a mother-daughter relationship. Longing for this type of relationship in my life, I have prayed for spiritual daughters and believe God has answered my request. I have had opportunities to encourage and mentor young women over the years as I worked as a volunteer small group leader in my church's youth ministry. But I have discovered that, although these relationships are special, they are not the same. There is a unique kinship or bond between a mother and a daughter that is hard to reproduce in other types of relationships. I know I will never be the mother of the bride and help my daughter adjust her wedding veil. And I will not be able to share that special moment with my daughter as her first baby is placed into her waiting arms. It hurts to know that these experiences will never be mine.

Just as I have ached to have daughters, I know that every single one of us will repeatedly experience some form of grief, ranging from minor inconveniences to devastating losses. I have known expectant mothers who dreamed of holding their unborn child only to have to face going home to an empty crib and the horrible chore of putting away unused baby clothes after their infant's premature death. I have watched my friends and family lose jobs, suffer physical injuries that ended their sports career, or have a spouse walk out after years of being married. My mother shared with me that my grandparents faithfully set aside one day of the week so that they could fast and pray for my uncle's healing from his congenital disorder of Down's Syndrome. And several years ago, a friend of mine shared how it felt to get the terrible phone call that her husband had unexpectedly died during a hunting trip. No one escapes the pain of loss, and mourning is a regular part of every person's life.

If grief and loss are a regular fixture of our lives, how are you to cope? We must embrace the pain of grief and learn to live with an expectant hope. We can take comfort knowing that God sees our losses and hears our cries of agony and disappointment. David, when captured by the Philistines in Gath, wrote, "Record my misery; list my tears on your scroll—are they not in your record?" (Psalm 56:8). God is not put off by or afraid of our cries of grief. Instead he longs for you to run to him so that he can console you.

In addition to taking comfort from God, you can also be encouraged that there is more to life than what you see here. We can live with a hope that there is life beyond death's door for we know Jesus Christ's crucifixion and resurrection has set us from free the tyranny of sin and death (1 Corinthians 15:54–56). You do not need to give in to despair because we have a confidence that one day all things will be set right. Death will not have the final say, and one day God will trade your mourning for joy and your despair for praise (Isaiah 61:3).

It hurt to watch my friend help her daughter get ready for her first dance. Although I dearly love my grown sons, there is an ache in my heart for that special mother-daughter relationship. However, I have prayerfully asked God to help me cope with this loss. I believe he has heard the longings of my heart and will satisfy it in a wonderful and surprising way someday. Meanwhile, I hold on to my God-given hope which allows me to take pleasure in my friend's joy.

PRACTICAL EXERCISES

1. Using individual pieces of paper, make a list of your unresolved losses. Include at least one detail about each one, such as how it has affected you. After you have finished recording your thoughts about each one, fold the slips of paper into tiny squares and imagine yourself placing them at the foot of God. In your mind's eye, see yourself leaving them there and listen for God's words of comfort and encouragement as you entrust them to him.

2. Most of us value self-sufficiency and strength. We might find it difficult or awkward to feel down, sad, or depressed. However, give yourself permission to experience your emotions. It is okay to cry, feel anger, or to have a limited amount of energy or motivation for outside interests or daily activities. Grief, like all emotions, will eventually come to an end. It might be very helpful to find a safe person to talk to about your struggle or loss, such as your pastor or a local Christian counselor.

3. It is well known in the counseling field that some of the best therapists are those with a personal familiarity with the particular treatment issue. At some point in your life have you suffered a crippling loss? How has God met you? How has the experience shaped you? Has God been using your healing in this area to encourage others? You might find that God gives you unique opportunities to support and help others facing similar circumstances.

OPTIONAL READINGS
1 Thessalonians 4:13–18
Revelation 21:1–5

DAILY DISCIPLINE EXERCISE

Read Psalm 30. David had known great pain. Later in his life his son Absalom revolted, killed his older brother who was heir to the throne, and tried to usurp David's monarchy, putting David once again on the run. Absalom's efforts were thwarted and he was killed, to David's great sorrow. Despite such upheaval and tragedy, David rejoiced in the security he found in God. He wrote this psalm as a dedication to the temple of God. Solomon would build the Temple years later, yet David joyously anticipated its construction. He loved God and celebrated his presence. How are you experiencing the security of God? How is God strengthening you with hope and clothing you with joy?

PRAYER

Dear God, My heart aches with grief sometimes. I know that life is filled with all types of losses: big ones and small ones. Please help me to place my hope in you. Encourage me when I feel overwhelmed by pain and remind me that you are making everything right and new.

Concluding Thoughts

Shortly before dawn Jesus went out to them, walking on the lake. When the disciples saw him walking on the lake, they were terrified. "It's a ghost," they said, and cried out in fear.

But Jesus immediately said to them: "Take courage! It is I. Don't be afraid." "Lord, if it's you," Peter replied, "tell me to come to you on the water."

"Come," he said.

Then Peter got down out of the boat, walked on the water and came toward Jesus. But when he saw the wind, he was afraid and, beginning to sink, cried out, "Lord, save me!"

Immediately Jesus reached out his hand and caught him. "You of little faith," he said, "why did you doubt?"

Matthew 14:25–31

Jesus had just learned his cousin, John the Baptist, was beheaded and tried to retreat to a quiet place in order to pray, but was having a hard time finding privacy due his popularity. After preaching and feeding five thousand people who had followed him, he withdrew again, this time by boat. Rowing to a quiet hillside, Jesus got out so that he could pray alone while the disciples stayed and waited in the boat. However, the wind picked up and the waves began to buffet the tiny boat, pushing it away from the shoreline. Once he had finished, instead of asking the waiting men to row back against the headwinds, Jesus walked across the choppy lake to re-join his group. The disciples became terrified since all they could see was a large shape moving towards them until Jesus called out and reassured them. Peter then responded to this disconcerting situation with the most outrageous request. He asked, "Lord if it is you…tell me to come to you on the water" (Matthew 14:28). Jesus agreed and Peter began to walk on the water toward Jesus until the weather conditions shook his faith and he took his eyes off Jesus.

Everyday we face these same circumstances. Just like the waves and wind on that lake, life gets rough and hard, threatening to overwhelm us. Jesus, however, comes and reassures us that he is near and that we are safe. And just as Jesus called out to his disciples to not be afraid, he urges you to trust him. And like Peter, Jesus encourages you to walk on the choppy waters of your difficult circumstances.

We are able to face scary and painful situations as long as we do not lose sight of him. However, if we focus on the conditions around us, we will become filled with fear. We will no longer be able to survive our circumstances but will be swallowed up by our anger, pain, grief, and anxiety.

Life will always be like that dark, choppy lake, but you can be victorious when you follow Jesus' instruction. He urges you to keep him first in your heart, to trust him with everything in your life, to follow him obediently no matter the cost, and to remain in him regardless how difficult life becomes. And, when you diligently work to keep your eyes on him, he promises to keep you safe. Life will never be easy, but you can be comforted that Jesus is guarding your eternal well being and gives you a guarantee that you will have an abundant life—now and for forever.

Conclusion

As a victim of early childhood abuse, I have struggled to understand why bad things happen to good people. Looking for answers, I read Corrie ten Boom's book, *The Hiding Place*, during middle school. The injustice of Corrie's experiences resonated with me. It helped me to realize that I wasn't the only one to suffer at the hands of others.

In her book, she recounted how she and her sister hid Jewish families who were fleeing from Nazi persecution. Unfortunately Corrie and her sister Betsy were eventually caught and imprisoned for their efforts. Corrie was miraculously released from prison, but the poor conditions led to Betsy's.[1]

Years later I happened to hear Dr. James Dobson interview Corrie ten Boom on his daily radio show, *Focus on the Family*. He asked her how she made sense of evil and suffering in the world. She replied that she believed God was weaving a tapestry of all the things that happen to us. She commented that she thought it would be a glorious picture, but, unfortunately, on this side of heaven, we are only able to see the backside with all its knots and tangled strings. From our perspective it looks like a mess.

Years later I thought of her answer as I sat across from a female client who, like me, had been abused. As I listened to this client's painful recount, I breathed a short prayer, "Lord, if you are creating a beautiful tapestry out of all our painful experiences, what picture are you making?" I didn't expect an answer; I was just trying to cope with the surge of hopelessness I was feeling. As I struggled to stay emotionally connected to my client's story, I suddenly had a vision. In my mind's eye I saw two hands holding a large tapestry that had been stretched between two long scrolls. The tapestry was slowly being raised before my eyes, but just as the picture would have become visible, the picture disappeared. At that moment I heard God's voice boom in my head as he said, "The Lamb!"

While researching the topic of Jesus as the Lamb for my second devotional book a few years ago, I discovered the personhood of Christ as the Lamb is the most frequently referenced name of Jesus in the book of Revelation, with over thirty mentions. Jesus is God's most Worthy, Slain Lamb (Revelation 5:12).

As I have considered the meaning of this vision, I am aware that human relationships are reciprocal and mutually affirming. We create an emotional feedback loop as we interact with each other. As we stare into each other's eyes, we observe the other person's reaction. We are aware of their feelings and opinions about our goodness, acceptability, and desirability. We either discard this information or unconsciously use it to shape our sense of worth. As a result, our sense of our self is potentially open for change and constantly being influenced by others' opinions of us. God, however, is not vulnerable to this same process. His sense of self isn't affected by the feedback he receives from us. He is complete within himself.

Since God isn't open to influence, then discussing God's attributes can feel impersonal. He behaves graciously, merciful, or patiently because God has and is all of those qualities. Our actions or needs don't improve or diminish his sense of himself. God is who he is. His love does not depend on our worthiness. As a result, his perfection and completeness as a person may create a sense that there is an emotional distance between us and him. He acts, and we are affected. The disparity of power might make him seem remote or cold, especially since it does not depend on our participation. Yet, I believe this is the farthest from the truth. God has a passionate nature and refers to himself as a "jealous God" (Exodus 34:14). God's infinite loving nature makes him capable of extending endless mercy and compassion, but it also opens him to suffering, for it impossible to love without also risking loss and experiencing the pain of rejection. Terence Fretheim explains, "By deciding to endure a wicked world, while continuing to open up the heart to that world, means that God has decided to take personal suffering upon God's own self.[2] Lois Tverberg in her book, *Walking in the Dust of Rabbi Jesus*, writes, "God is *not* indifferent or disinterested; rather he's an Arab father who is crushed by his son's apparent lack of love. God is a mother bear who roars a warning if you get too close to her cubs. God is a jilted boyfriend who's beside himself when he spots his true love on another guy's arm. Israel's God is not less emotional than you are; he is even *more*."[3] God is your most passionate pursuer and is deeply invested in events of your life.

As I have considered the meaning of the tapestry vision, I have come to the conclusion that God takes and uses all of our pain and suffering to wake us up to our need for him. When life is comfortable and we feel satisfied, we often become spiritually complacent. Our ease lulls us into believing we have enough and spiritual issues can wait. This is a lie, especially since sin has twisted our nature and we are facing eternal separation from God. God, in his infinite love and mercy, wakes us up with pain. He uses it to draw our attention to our *need* for him. In that moment, our desperate state and our need can remind us, God is near. He is present and ever available.

As a fellow sufferer, I have come to the conclusion that if pain's sole purpose was to make us mindful of God, then it has served us well, but I suspect there is another objective. I believe God also was sharing in that vision that Jesus is intimately involved in the drama of yours and my life and that all of our experiences become a part of his story. Some day you will see this beautiful tapestry of Christ. And, in the story of that picture, you will once again see evidence of God's nearness. He is here, right now. Right beside you. You have been never forgotten.

Sources

Chapter 1- Our Mysterious & Good God

[1] Tozer, A.W., *The Knowledge of the Holy*. (HarperOne, 1961), 49.

[2] Lewis, C.S., *The Lion, The Witch, and the Wardrobe*. (HarperCollins Children's Books, 2000).

[3] Tozer, A.W., *The Knowledge of the Holy*. (HarperOne, 1961), 82.

[4] ibid, 83.

[5] Lewis, Thomas, Amini, Fari, and Lannon, Richard, *A General Theory of Love*. (Vintage Books, 2000), 83.

[6] ibid, 89.

Chapter 2- When Life Doesn't Make Sense

[1] "Behnam Irani," *PresenTruth Ministries*. http://presenttruthmn.com/behnam-irani/ (September 19, 2013).

[2] Crosby, Fanny, *Blessed Assurance*. (1873).

[3] American Sunday-School Union, *The Sunday-School World*. 40, Issue 8, (1900).

[4] Boyd, Gregory, *God at War: The Bible & Spiritual Conflict*. (IVP Academic, 1997), 199.

Chapter 3- Our Psychological Need for God

[1] Calhoun, Adele Ahlberg, *Spiritual Disciplines Handbook: Practices That Transform Us*. (IVP Books, 2005).

[2] Karen, Robert, *Becoming Attached: First Relationships and How They Shape Our Capacity to Love*. (Oxford University Press, USA, 1998).

[3] "Heinz Kohut," International Association for Psychoanalytic Self Psychology. http://www.psychologyoftheself.com/kohut/strozier1.php (September 19, 2013).

Chapter 4- Comfort in God

[1] Lewis, Thomas, Amini, Fari, and Lannon, Richard, *A General Theory of Love.* (Vintage Books, 2000), 61.

[2] Tozer, A.W., *The Pursuit of God/The Pursuit of Man.* (Christian Publications, Inc. 1993), 14.

[3] ibid, 18.

Conclusion

[1] "Lessons by Corrie Ten Boom," *How Shall They Hear Without a Preacher? http://www.amazinggracebaptistchurchkjv.com/Download60.html* (January 29, 2010).

[2] Fretheim, Terence. *The Suffering of God.* (Philadelphia: Fortress, 1984), 112.

[3] Tverberg, Lois. *Walking in the Dust of Rabbi Jesus: How the Jewish Word of Jesus Can Change Your Life.* (Zondervan, 2013), 180.

CONNECT WITH THE AUTHOR

https://kerrymcavoyphd.com